The
GREAT NADAR

NADAR. élevant la Photographie à la hauteur de l'Art

The
GREAT NADAR

THE MAN BEHIND
THE CAMERA

ADAM BEGLEY

TIM
DUGGAN
BOOKS

NEW YORK

Library of Congress Cataloging-in-Publication Data
Names: Begley, Adam, author.
Title: The great Nadar: the man behind the camera / Adam Begley.
Description: First edition. | New York: Tim Duggan Books, 2017. |
Includes index.
Identifiers: LCCN 2016045382 (print) | LCCN 2016047857 (ebook) |
ISBN 9781101902608 (hardcover) | ISBN 9781101902622 (trade pbk.) |
ISBN 9781101902615 (ePub)
Subjects: LCSH: Nadar, Félix, 1820–1910. |
Photographers—France—Biography.
Classification: LCC TR140.N24 B45 2017 (print) | LCC TR140.N24 (ebook) |
DDC 770.92 [B]—dc23
LC record available at https://lccn.loc.gov/2016045382

ISBN 978-1-101-90260-8
Ebook ISBN 978-1-101-90261-5

Printed in the United States of America

Book design by Lauren Dong
Jacket design by Christopher Brand
Jacket photograph: Félix Nadar/Bibliothèque Nationale de France
Illustration credits appear on page 237.

1 3 5 7 9 10 8 6 4 2

First Edition

To Louis and Anka

CONTENTS

NADAR ALOFT

T HE YEAR IS 1865, OR POSSIBLY 1864. THE PLACE IS A
four-story building on the south side of the boulevard des
Capucines, between La Madeleine and the Opéra, stroll-
ing distance from the epicenter of fashionable Paris. If you look up,
you'll see near the top of the facade of number 35 a name in giant
script: *Nadar,* signed with a flourish in red glass tubing, the letters
ten feet high, the whole trademark fifty feet long. At night the sign
is gaslit, a garish crimson beacon advertising the studio of the most
famous photographer in France. Nadar is a celebrity, renowned
not only for his portraits of eminent contemporaries but also for
his caricatures, his writings, his radical politics, and his daredevil
exploits as a balloonist. Today he will be calling upon several of
his talents at once: he is at work on a portrait of himself as an aeronaut, a task that combines self-exposure with self-promotion and
self-caricature. His motives, like almost all motives, are mixed.
The photograph will advertise his art, promote the cause of human
flight—the cause closest to his heart (at the moment)—and serve
a specific commercial purpose: generate publicity for a memoir of
his most notorious ballooning adventure. But he's chronically incapable of suppressing the artistic ambition that has shaped his photographic career—that is, the urge to capture in every portrait an
intimate and compelling psychological likeness. This photo will be
a triumph.

The preparation is elaborate. A balloon gondola, a wicker basket about the size of a steamer trunk, is draped in paisley fabric

and suspended from the steel rafters of the studio's glass ceiling. Equipped for flight, complete with grapnel anchor hooked to the side, the gondola must appear to hang from a vast aerostat hovering above, just beyond the frame of the photo. A canvas backdrop of painted clouds gives the illusion that the basket is floating high in the sky—such is the low-tech fakery of early photography. One of Nadar's assistants attends to the camera, a bulky box mounted on four spidery wooden legs. Covered with a heavy black cloth, the young man peers through the lens at his boss and releases the shutter. Exposure time is a few seconds, so the celebrated aeronaut must hold his pose.

And there he is, aloft, a dapper Nadar in top hat, black coat, and floppy cravat, a jaunty tartan blanket tossed over his shoulder—a dandy of the air. Billowing out from under the brim of the hat, his hair is long, thick, and curly. His mustache, bushy, unkempt, is a reminder of his bohemian youth. Because the photo is black and white, turned sepia with age, we miss the effect of his coloring: hair and mustache are fiery red. Seated in the gondola, elbows out, shoulders square, he's a solid, capable presence. He radiates composure and serious intent, as though he were charged with making important observations from a great height—in one hand he clutches an impressive pair of binoculars. His purposeful demeanor conveys calm in the face of danger: he is a man on a mission, going it alone.

An uncropped print of the photo comically undercuts that message: at the edge of the image, a few feet from the gondola, another assistant stands idly by, clearly unmoved by his boss's simulated aerial adventure. The bored look on this employee's face brings Nadar down to earth with a bump. Our hero is not drifting along with the clouds; the bottom of the basket is barely a yard above the studio floor. His long legs are tucked up inside the gondola; layers of bulky clothing and an assertive pose disguise his gangly frame—he's about as solid as a broomstick. As for the observations he might be making from on high, he's in truth very nearsighted, his prominent, widely spaced eyes too weak for reconnaissance. (Look closely, and you can see his spectacles hanging on a ribbon around his neck.) Though he is in fact a brave man, in most other respects the impression he's pushing to make is false. There's never been anything calm about Nadar: his close friend Baudelaire singled him out as "the most astonishing expression of vitality." Exuberant, agitated, impetuous, horrified by tedium and relentlessly

and infectiously gregarious, Nadar in his mid-forties is cheerfully scattered, still childlike in his roaring enthusiasms. He means well—but many in his army of companions know that they can't always rely on him.

Nadar would be the first to laugh at the yawning gap between the pose—the image he plans to project—and the reality captured in the uncropped version of the photo. And yet ballooning is to him quite literally a matter of life and death. He's determined to put before the public a confidence-inspiring portrait of himself as an intrepid aeronaut: he must appear resolute and in control, a pioneer exploring a new frontier, advancing a sacred cause—what he called *le droit au vol* (the right to flight).

His pose in another photograph taken the same day is even more intense. Rigidly upright, he stares with wide bright eyes, his fixed gaze almost messianic. Is it the future he sees in the distance, a glorious tomorrow when all mankind will be triumphantly airborne? (The hallmarks of modernity, he believed, were "photography, electricity, and aeronautics.") A fellow aeronaut, his wife Ernestine, is in the basket with him, the tartan blanket now wrapped around her slender frame. She looks up at her husband's face with uneasy devotion, loyal but wary.

Wary with good cause. Ernestine was the only woman among the nine passengers aboard Nadar's humongous balloon, *Le Géant* (The Giant), when it crashed spectacularly on Monday, October 19, 1863—a disaster dramatic enough to earn Nadar newspaper headlines on both sides of the Atlantic. It's a tribute to his powers of persuasion that he was able to convince his young wife to climb back into a balloon basket, even with the basket hanging in the safety of the studio.

Ernestine's ordeal aboard *Le Géant* began with an auspicious launch. This was the balloon's second outing, and a huge crowd, tens of thousands, assembled on the Champ de Mars on Sunday afternoon to watch while it was inflated with more than two hundred thousand cubic feet of gas. Next to it was a balloon of conventional size, a masterstroke on Nadar's part. When *Le Géant* rose to its full height of nearly two hundred feet—about twelve stories—it was visible from all over the city; it towered above the smaller balloon. *Le Géant*'s gondola was a little house made of wicker, a cabin with a half-dozen separate compartments, including kitchen and lavatory. There was a separate compartment for the storage of wine and champagne. On hand to witness the liftoff were Emperor Napoléon III and his guest the king of Greece. If Nadar was gratified by the presence of these potentates, he carefully disguised his feelings; he was reluctant to compromise his radical socialist and republican loyalties.

As the sun sank in the west, *Le Géant* rose up magnificent and passed swiftly over the Seine, past the boulevard des Capucines, gaining altitude over Montmartre, newly annexed to the city, and sailing out over the countryside, propelled by the wind in a northeasterly direction, toward Brussels.

Crew and passengers, some of them seasoned aeronauts, some novices, ate dinner on the upper deck, en plein air. During the night, they passed over Belgium and the Netherlands and at dawn found themselves drifting eastward into Germany. Near Hanover, it was decided that they would attempt a landing.

As they descended, they realized that the wind was now a stiff gale, and their rate of travel dangerously speedy. Worse, the crew couldn't manage to let enough gas escape to deflate the enormous balloon—nor did they have the means to make it rise again. They had no choice, in other words, but to go through with what promised to be a high-risk landing. The grapnel anchors proved useless: the lines snapped at once. Whipped along by the wind, the partially deflated balloon dragged the gondola across the open countryside at more than twenty miles an hour, the cabin smacking into the ground, rising up once more as high as forty yards, and smashing down again, the terrified passengers hanging on desperately, convinced that violent death was unavoidable.

The balloon—Nadar described it as a "crazed comet"—careened onward for almost half an hour, covering mile after mile, crossing a railway line and narrowly avoiding an oncoming train, splashing through a wide stream, before clattering into a small wood. One by one crew and passengers were thrown clear, until only Nadar and Ernestine remained, clinging to each other and to the leather grips on the wicker railing of the upper deck—then they too were ejected, just before the stand of trees finally halted the balloon's catastrophic progress.

Incredibly, no one died, although all nine passengers were hurt, just one of them seriously, a young poet who was nearly flayed alive and broke his leg as well. Nadar's legs were badly bruised and abraded, but he suffered only a hairline fracture. Also severely bruised, Ernestine coughed up alarming quantities of blood but made a rapid and full recovery. A fellow passenger later commended her "magnificent sang-froid" during the harrowing half-hour of the epically botched landing.

The weird and wonderful fact is that Nadar had dreamed up his "monster balloon" to demonstrate the limitations of ballooning. He had become convinced of the impossibility of navigating a craft lighter than air. A balloon moves *with* the air, propelled this way and that by the shifting currents. He wanted to cut *through* the air. The future, he believed, belonged to "aero-locomotives" such as helicopters and airplanes. *Le Géant* was built for the express purpose of raising money to fund the construction of a heavier-than-air machine, an aircraft that would "kill" ballooning—preferably before ballooning killed him and his wife and left their young son an orphan.

Part damage control, part devil-may-care defiance, the studio photographs of Nadar the aeronaut coolly in charge of an evidently stable balloon, surveying the scene imperturbably from a prodigious height, are propaganda, part of a strategy that had taken shape even before he launched and crashed *Le Géant*. The calamitous landing, he knew before the wreckage was cleared, would serve his purpose by exciting public interest. Catastrophe sells—so he commissioned a drawing of the perilous moment when balloon and train seemed on a collision course.

Reproduced in magazines and newspapers around the world, it was the frontispiece of *Mémoires du Géant,* one of the two books (the other was *Le Droit au vol*) he was already hoping to promote when he climbed into a balloon basket in his studio with a top hat on his head.

But it's the outtake, the uncropped photo with the bored assistant looking on, that achieves Nadar's artistic ambition. Here the beauty and mad glory of his contradictions come to life. The artist, the publicist, and the adventurer are conspiring, gambling everything to will the future into being.

FÉLIX

H E WASN'T BORN NADAR; IT WAS A NICKNAME BE-
stowed when he was a very young man, a measure of his
popularity with a new group of friends. The nickname
became a badge of his emerging public identity: he used *Nadar* as a
nom de plume, then as a logo. Protected by court order, the pseudonym was his trademark and became, in the last decades of his
long life, his most valuable property.

The name on his birth certificate was Gaspard-Félix Tournachon. His parents called him Félix. It would be pleasingly tidy to di-
vide his private and public life between the two names, but in truth
he used them more or less interchangeably from age twenty on.
Letters to his mother he invariably signed Félix, but letters to his
wife and his brother he sometimes signed Nadar. To colleagues and
acquaintances he was almost always Nadar, as he was to friends.

The pseudonym was an emblem of his success, and then of his
celebrity; from early on the name *Tournachon* had darker associations: it was freighted with a complex family history shadowed
by madness and failure, played out against a bloody backdrop of
national turmoil. His father, Victor Tournachon, born in Lyon in
1771, scion of a venerable Lyonnais family, is listed on his son's
birth certificate as a merchant. More specifically, Victor was a publisher, like his father before him: a printer and a bookseller. If that
sounds comfortably bourgeois, settled, and secure, remember that
in 1789, when Victor was eighteen, France was turned upside down
by the Revolution and that purveyors of the printed word were able

to do business only when the political climate and censorship laws allowed it. The Tournachon family was sympathetic to change and negotiated the terrifying and disorienting upheaval of the last decade of the eighteenth century—particularly brutal and confused in Lyon—without losing their property or their heads.

A child of the Romantic era, tall and good-looking, Victor was an idealist, faithful to Robespierre's revolutionary motto *"Liberté, Égalité, Fraternité."* He had radical ideas about how society should be reformed, and believed that marriage was incompatible with true love (and *liberté*). In 1817, when he fell in love with a twenty-four-year-old from a bourgeois family, he stuck to his principles and decamped to Paris with his young sweetheart. The couple lived together—unmarried—at 195, rue Saint-Honoré, willing exiles from the tyranny of social convention. Victor established himself in his old line of work, publishing a best-selling volume, Félicité de Lamennais's treatise *Essay on Indifference in Matters of Religion*, and early works by Alexandre Dumas.

Because his parents weren't married, Félix is listed on the birth certificate as a *fils naturel* (natural son), a polite French term meaning he was illegitimate. His mother is listed as Thérèse Maillet, of independent means. Those means were unfortunately slender: her husband's principled stand against matrimony meant that her family in Lyon did not offer a dowry. Soon after Félix was born (on April 6, 1820, in the evening, after a difficult delivery), the family moved to 26, rue de Richelieu, a few steps from the Palais-Royal. Six years later—by which time Félix's father was fifty-five years old, his mother thirty-two, and his baby brother, Adrien, just one—his parents were legally wed. This about-face came as Victor's once prosperous business began to show alarming signs of decline. The family moved to the Left Bank, to 45, rue Saint-André-des-Arts.

In 1830 Charles X was deposed by the July Revolution, and Louis-Philippe d'Orléans installed as the new king of France. In a bleak climate for booksellers, Victor's fortunes suffered further collapse; three years later his business lay in ruins. The proximate cause was the spiraling cost of publishing a twenty-five-volume encyclopedia of French law—just the kind of quixotic project guaranteed to appeal to the high-minded but impractical Victor, who lingered in Paris for several years before retreating, in failing health, humbled by his losses and fearful for his sanity, to Lyon. As Félix wrote many years later, "A good man, my father wasn't born to be in business any more than I was born to be a bishop." Thérèse and young Adrien accompanied Victor to Lyon, to his brother's house. Thirteen-year-old Félix stayed behind in the capital, alone.

For several years he had been boarding at a succession of schools in Paris and just outside the city in Versailles. At the time of his parents' departure, he was lodged at an establishment associated with the Collège Bourbon (now the Lycée Condorcet) run by a kind and forbearing man named Charles Augeron. An inconsistent pupil, Félix had shown flashes of brilliance but was also prone to unexplained lapses. He was playful and sensitive, well liked and generally happy, charming in letters to his parents and in surviving fragments of a youthful diary. Several of his schoolmates became lifelong friends.

At age sixteen, he was already exhibiting signs of a fascination with literary life and celebrity. He wrote to his mother in Lyon asking for Dumas's address and a pretext for visiting the newly famous author. The boy's interest was sparked when he saw a portrait of Dumas hanging in Madame Augeron's sitting room. That same year Félix contributed to the school's student newspaper a short story called "And Yet She Was Born Virtuous," in which a young man describes his attempt to rehabilitate a prostitute. Félix later claimed that the story, his first, prompted the school to ban the student newspaper.

With the departure of his family, both his discipline and his academic record suffered. He was mixed up in every kind of schoolyard scrape, sometimes as culprit, sometimes as scapegoat. Then, messing around with some newfangled chemical matches, he somehow blew up the stove in his classroom, causing minor damage and inflicting minor burns—an incident too serious for Augeron to ignore. Félix was expelled and found himself living on the streets for several days, until the good-hearted schoolmaster took pity and allowed him to return.

The baccalaureate, a diploma introduced by Napoléon at the beginning of the century, would have been Félix's chance to show that his intermittent displays of academic excellence were no fluke—but he never took the exam. His studies were interrupted by the death of his father in a Lyon hospital on August 8, 1837, the cause an "organic illness of the brain." According to Adrien, age twelve at the time, the end was horrible.

Félix left Paris to rejoin what remained of his family. Nearly destitute, Thérèse had taken refuge in her sister's house. Félix enrolled in a Lyon medical school with the idea that the profession would earn him enough to provide for his mother and brother. In his spare time, he wrote for a couple of reputable local journals. His first published contribution, a short story laced with gothic clichés, appeared in *Journal du commerce et des théâtres de Lyon* in two installments in the spring of 1838. Next he turned to theater reviews, in which he made it abundantly clear that he considered Lyon audiences hopelessly provincial. He was homesick for the capital (a friend once remarked that he was "Parisian to the tips of his fingernails"), and within months he was back where he belonged, still studying medicine but increasingly drawn to journalism.

He was only fitfully engaged by his studies. In a short story, he described with gleeful horror the dissection of corpses, young anatomy students plunging bloody hands into chopped-up cadavers, fishing about in the viscera to retrieve this organ or that, sawing through skulls to peek at brains, all the while singing obscene songs and laughing uproariously. Intrigued by science and excited by the promise of scientific advancement, Félix was naturally curious about the latest medical discoveries. His father's fatal illness sharpened that curiosity—and his father's bankruptcy made the thought of a lucrative profession seem appealing. But his temperament wasn't suited to the rigor and discipline of scientific training. Journalism, a gateway to literary life, though less respectable than medicine and less remunerative, proved irresistible.

Even before leaving Lyon, Félix had been busy trying to secure part-time employment with a magazine in the capital. As soon as he arrived back in Paris, he went to work for a seemingly prosperous publication called *Journal des dames*—which folded less than a year later. This abrupt collapse set the tone for the next dozen years.

Having abandoned his medical studies, he threw himself into the hectic world of start-up newspapers and little magazines, writing for the *Revue et gazette des théâtres*, doing odd jobs, and scribbling in the company of a motley assortment of aspiring poets and painters, most of them, like him, young and penniless.

When he was in his early forties, Félix would present the world with a self-portrait in the form of an extended verbal onslaught. Allowing for relentless facetiousness and pride in perversity, it's a weirdly accurate portrait of the young man eager to make his way in the capital. As implied in the rant, middle-aged Nadar resembled teenaged Félix in most respects—whatever maturity he achieved came later. Here's our hero, then, looking at himself in the mirror and writing down his impressions in typically rushed, headlong prose:

A real daredevil, always looking for tides to swim against, braving public opinion, unreconciled to any sense of order, boasting of having reached his forties when everyone can tell that he's only twelve or thirteen at most;—a dabbler, laughing on one side, pinching on the other, rude to the point of calling things by their name and people too, and never having missed the opportunity to talk about rope in a house where someone has been hanged or ought to be hanged. Without moderation or restraint, exaggerated in all things, impatient in discussion, violent in speech, obstinate rather than persevering, enthusiastic about nothing, skeptical of everything, a mistrustful embracer of all quarrels, a picker-up of people who are down, always on the move and therefore stepping on everybody's toes, which those who have corns will not forgive.— Imprudent to the point of temerity, and reckless to the point of folly, having passed his life throwing himself out sixth-floor windows just to land on his feet, furnishing legends for the idle onlooker, and compelled despite himself by relentless good fortune to make the most benign grind their teeth, since he's never succeeded in diluting himself entirely.—A noisy personality, engrossing, embarrassing, annoying, exciting curiosity, which annoys him,—and consequently a target on every street corner; a born rebel vis-à-vis any yoke, impatient with propriety, skittish as a hare at the door of any house where one doesn't put one's feet up, having never learned to answer a letter until two years later, and—so that nothing's missing, not even one last physical flaw, to top it off, to show the extent of his attractive virtues and to gather round him several more good friends—pushing myopia to the point of blindness, and consequently struck with the most impertinent forgetfulness in front of every face he hasn't seen at least twenty-five times no more than six inches from the end of his nose.

What more can I say—I could go on and on—about a fellow so lacking in brains that he never even had the slightest common sense . . . and didn't take himself seriously for one moment in his life or begin to think of himself as someone so that others could be persuaded to do the same.

And he added, not yet exhausted by his simultaneously self-lacerating and self-congratulatory tirade, that he was every father-in-law's worst nightmare, and that his most shameful shortcoming was a hatred of boredom.

Others said about him that no one ever had more friends than Nadar. His mentor Charles Philipon once wryly observed that for Nadar's capacious heart, "eight thousand more friends or eight thousand fewer is no big deal."

LA VIE DE BOHÈME

"Bohemia is a necessary stage of the artistic life,
it is the prologue to the Academy, to the State Hospital,
or to the public morgue."
—HENRY MURGER, 1851

IN JUNE 1838, AFTER HIS BRIEF, UNHAPPY STINT IN LYON, Félix returned to Paris, a pale beanpole teenager with prominent blue eyes and orange hair. He was on his own, a de facto orphan, separated from the grieving Thérèse, who remained in Lyon with Adrien. From age eighteen to twenty-five, Félix lived by himself in a succession of cramped rooms, most often in the Quartier Latin. Whenever possible he gathered around himself a menagerie of animals: dogs, cats, birds, even monkeys. With people, his talent was for translating sudden intimacy into a more enduring attachment, cemented by honesty, loyalty, fellow feeling, and high spirits. In cahoots with a pal, his eccentric brilliance ran wild, energy and affection overwhelming any reserve on his companion's part. For some, it was too much; the force of his personality, his exuberance, seemed to them more of an assault than an overture.

His network of friends—dense in Paris and eventually spread out across France and abroad—became his surrogate family. They are the very same hungry, garret-dwelling would-be artists made famous by Puccini's opera *La Bohème,* which was itself based on *Scènes de la vie de bohème,* a collection of atmospheric tales about the noble suffering of impoverished artists that became a literary sensation in the early 1850s. The author was Henry Murger, sometimes known as "the first bohemian." (Why bohemian? Because Murger and his pals lived like vagabonds or gypsies, and gypsies were thought to have come from Bohemia—or Egypt, hence gypsy.) Henry Murger was a close friend of the footloose young Félix. As was everybody else.

To the poet Théodore de Banville, Félix seemed to already know every living being when he himself was barely born. Not quite—but his cheerful, agitated good humor, broadcast by an unstoppable flow of banter, gave that impression. "He dazzles you every minute with the thousand facets of his brilliant conversation," reported another friend, Charles Bataille, who described a torrent of speech, rich in images—"turbulent, unexpected, terrifying like the knives of Chinese jugglers." Félix made a habit of addressing everyone, young or old, rich or poor, with the informal *tu;* his aim was to bond instantly, if at all possible.

A few of his friends he had met as a schoolboy, among them Charles Asselineau, Baudelaire's first biographer, who also studied medicine briefly before turning to writing. Some were colleagues who worked at the string of little magazines where Félix earned a meager living, first with his writing and then with his caricatures. Other friends he met in the muddy streets of the Quartier Latin or in the Jardin du Luxembourg; they gathered in restaurants, in theaters, in art galleries, in squalid, overcrowded attic rooms. Or in cafés, their names a roll call of nineteenth-century establishments: Voltaire, Tabourey, de l'Europe, Dagneaux, Le Progrès, Momus, Le La Rochefoucauld, Le Divan le Peletier. Félix wasn't loyal to any particular café; he flitted from one to another, always certain to find some old pals—or to make new ones.

The nickname *Nadar* was bestowed by Auguste Lefranc, a lawyer who quit the law to devote himself to writing vaudeville comedies. Lefranc claimed credit for transforming *Tournachon* into *Tournadard.* Within months, *Tournadard* was shortened to *Nadard;* the final *d* dropped off for good in about 1849. As a young man, Félix signed letters "Tournach" and "Nadar-chon"—the new name evolved gradually and playfully. Already in 1839 he received letters addressed to Nadar—but it was nearly a decade before he would use it regularly as his pen name. (Many of the articles and illustrations in the small magazines were in any case unsigned.) His family name faded from view only slowly.

A couple of years after his return to the capital, with spare change jangling in his pocket (at the time he was earning a steady salary at a weekly newspaper), he made an unabashed bid for notoriety. Comically flaunting his ambition, he invited the many young people he knew—along with certain celebrated characters he wished to know—to a *fête champêtre,* to be held on a Friday night in late November 1840. The festivities offer a peek into a corner of Parisian society navigated with considerable flair by this audacious young man.

The very idea of announcing and organizing a *fête champêtre,* a kind of fancy garden party popularized in the eighteenth century, and holding it in his small room in the middle of Paris (at 88, rue Montmartre, a thoroughly urban environment) was already tongue-in-cheek, as even a glance at the lithographed invitation made obvious. The archaic spelling of the event ("Feste Champestre") set the tone, as did the assumed name of the host: "M. le vicomte de la Tour Nadard." This noble personage boasted of the brilliance of the guests who would be attending his soirée, assuring his invitees, "There will be *decent* women."

The program of events, also lithographed, touted a sequence of outlandish entertainments including swings, clay pigeon shooting, fireworks, and racy *tableaux vivants*. The guests lured by this elaborate nonsense spilled out of Félix's room—rechristened "l'Élysée Nadard"—down the staircase and out onto the sidewalk of the rue Montmartre. A midnight surprise was promised, preceded by "odious dances," "savage cries," and "the incongruous personal hallucinations of witty authors." The nature of the surprise remains a mystery—but whatever it was, Félix had made his mark. According to an awed Banville, just seventeen at the time, the party succeeded brilliantly, coming off "without a hitch." At the tender age of twenty, Félix had established himself as a master publicist, his self-promotion sweetened by self-parody.

Over the next dozen years, the label *bohemian* gained currency, popularized by Murger's serialized stories, one of which featured a soirée unmistakably patterned on the extravagant frolic at the Élysée Nadard. With his energy and enthusiasm, Félix helped set the tone for this loose-knit community of feckless dreamers and would-be artists. In that sense, he had a hand in shaping the whole notion of bohemianism, especially insofar as it implied a thumbing of the nose at bourgeois attitudes, a carefree embrace of eccentricity, and a reflexive political radicalism more romantic than practical. He continued to live like a bohemian until he married, in 1854, and even afterward remained wholly sympathetic to bohemian attitudes. Long after he became famous and acquired the trappings of a bourgeois life, his contemporaries continued to associate the name *Nadar* with bohemia.

Whereas Murger, especially in the stage adaptation of his stories, celebrated the picturesque charm of his bohemian comrades and the nobility of their artistic aspirations, Félix for the most part resisted the tug of nostalgia. He was more likely to harp on the hunger and hardship he and his friends endured in their obscure, garret-hopping days. He remembered cold and want, having nowhere to sleep and nothing but raw potatoes to eat. Seen in the context of chronic poverty punctuated by days of utter destitution, his *fête champêtre* seems a gesture of lively defiance.

On a damp, chilly day in November 1843, a fellow bohemian, Charles Barbara, saw a forlorn Félix walking in the street. Barbara was so struck by the abject figure Félix cut that he wrote about it in a letter to their mutual friend André Léon-Noël, another bohemian, also habitually broke, who had played a prominent part in the *fête champêtre* three years earlier:

> Fortune was no longer smiling on him. With a gray hat on, a little green frock coat, hands in his pockets, pipe in his mouth, a pale complexion, his head philosophically bowed to the ground, he seemed sunk in painful meditations. He wasn't alone. Following in his footsteps . . . a skinny long-haired spaniel, looking stretched out like his master, head and tail drooping. . . . They passed on one side of the street, I on the other, and I didn't dare accost them—for their sake, not mine. All joking aside, I felt overcome with pity for them.

A more cheerful, and certainly more colorful, recollection of Félix down and out came from Étienne Carjat, a successful journalist and photographer who would follow a career path similar to our hero's. Carjat told an unforgettable though obviously exaggerated story about being young and newly arrived in Paris and going to see Nadar, who was living in penury: Félix hadn't stirred from his bed for two months, having no clothes to go out in. His mistress had pantaloons and yellow leather boots she wore to the Opéra Ball. The two of them had a passion for oysters, and the discarded shells carpeted the floor of the room. Carjat said he had never seen such dire poverty.

Oysters also figure in an anecdote well polished by Charles Bataille, who was living in 1849 on the rue Neuve-des-Martyrs (now the rue Manuel), in a mezzanine apartment with a balcony. On the opposite side of the street, on the fifth floor, lived a distinctive neighbor: a tall, spindly character who wore a scarlet jacket and used to climb down the outside of the building "like a skinny cat," possibly to avoid the concierge or possibly just for the fun of it. One day Bataille was on his way to a concert when his top hat was targeted by a volley of oyster shells. Looking up, he saw on the fifth-floor terrace the neighbor in the scarlet jacket rocking with laughter.

This rude introduction led to a lightning friendship: a furious Bataille sent up his calling card with a message scrawled on the back: "Sir, you drop your household garbage on my head, — I send you my address." The reply was instantaneous, a note from Félix that read, "Why didn't you warn me that you work with words? Here we buy them, so come on up!" Curiosity mingling with anger, Bataille climbed the stairs to the fifth floor. After two minutes of conversation, Félix was stuffing little balls of bread into Bataille's ears; after fifteen minutes, he was calling him *imbéchille* ("imbecile" with a lisp), a favorite term of endearment; after a week, the two were inseparable.

Rue Neuve-des-Martyrs was in the Quartier de Rochechouart, just below Montmartre. Bataille described the street as populated with bohemians and women who, as he put it, "were likely to lead you quickly and directly to the definitive goal of all human experience." In other words, Félix felt right at home. This was Paris before the transformations wrought by Baron Haussmann and his broad, clean, gaslit boulevards. Narrow, crowded streets without sidewalks, filthy and muddy, were the rule in the neighborhoods bohemians could afford. At one point in the mid-1840s, Félix was living in the Faubourg Saint-Germain, in a small furnished room on the top floor of a building on the modest rue des Canettes. Directly across the street, in similar digs, perched Henry Murger and several of his cronies. They found it convenient to converse by shouting from window to window, three stories above the street. Down below, passersby were treated to a stream of gossip about girls (the name Anna was much bandied about: at the time several of them, including Félix, happened to have lovers named Anna); laments over the familiar lack of funds; and ferocious arguments about aesthetics, especially between Félix and the fiery Antoine Fauchery, who later joined Félix and his brother on a mad excursion to Poland (and later still took up photography and established a studio in Melbourne, Australia). According to Félix, these discussions would usually end with a barrage of insults and the slamming of windows. Little groups would gather in the street to enjoy the free entertainment up above.

Almost all his bohemian friends, even the few possessed of true talent, are now forgotten. The most brilliant exceptions are Charles Baudelaire and Gérard de Nerval. They're remembered for their writing, especially their poetry, but it's thanks to photographs signed Nadar that we have a clear sense of what they looked like. Félix made a series of portraits of Baudelaire, an eloquent succession of images that shows the poet aging over the course of about eight years; we see him refining his persona and coping with notoriety. (The later portraits were made after 1857, when *Les Fleurs du mal* was judged in court to be "an outrage to public morals.") Félix claimed that Nerval sat for him only once—just days

before the poet's suicide in January 1855—but there's evidence that Nerval visited the studio in November 1854 and on previous occasions. The Nadar photos show (or are we fooled by hindsight?) a man with sorrowful eyes whose brave mustache hides a crumpled mouth. In his stained fingers he holds the chewed end of an extinguished cigar. Several years earlier Nerval had written that photography destroys illusions by "confronting each face with the mirror of truth." In this case, the mirror revealed a man stripped of hope.

Félix may have met Nerval as early as 1839, but it was not until nearly a decade later that they worked together for a few months at the offices of a daily newspaper. Félix was too young to have known Nerval in his twenties and thirties when he was busy squandering his inheritance. He lived, for a happy moment, in a kind of bohemian commune on the rue du Doyenné, where he and his fellow poet Théophile Gautier gave a legendary party that was the pattern for Félix's *fête champêtre*. Nerval's later years, punctuated by mental breakdowns, were more solitary and somber. In 1847, when Félix wrote a brief prose portrait of his friend, he called him "gentle, naïve, benevolent, affectionate. If once you see him, I defy you not to love him, and not to look for ways to be agreeable to him, or useful."

In the popular imagination, Nerval remains the arch-eccentric who took a pet lobster, Thibault, for a stroll in the gardens of the Palais-Royal, the leash a length of blue silk ribbon. The poet's precocious success (at age eighteen he published an acclaimed translation of Goethe's *Faust*) and the testimony of those who considered him a genius (Alexandre Dumas and Baudelaire among them), meant that his death provoked astonishment in literary Paris. Félix, when he wrote at length about Nerval's demise, focused neither on his eccentricity nor on his literary talent but rather on his kindly nature, charm, and refined and delicate sensibility. He had killed himself, Félix insisted, neither because he was mad nor because he was poor (though he had only ten centimes in his pocket and his clothes were threadbare). Convinced that he had exhausted his capacity to earn money with his pen, and unwilling to accept generosity from his friends that he couldn't repay, he refused even the most discreet offers of help. No, Félix concluded, Nerval "died of honor."

Félix felt the suicide keenly. In his imagination, he relived the cold night in January when his friend trudged through the snow to the narrow rue de la Vieille Lanterne. Halfway down the dismal alley was a window secured by seven iron bars. Félix imagined poor Gérard stopping there and with swollen fingers tying his laces to one of the bars—the fourth bar—and hanging himself, his feet barely off the ground.

Obsessing over these morbid details, making numerous "pilgrimages" to the rue de la Vieille Lanterne, Félix was indulging his gothic sensibilities. In what feels like an embellishment inspired by Edgar Allan Poe or by Nerval himself, he even claimed that on his visits to the dark, damp alley, he often met a stranger, a silent man absorbed in thought. The neighborhood was slated for demolition (part of the relentless modernization of central Paris), and Félix saw this mysterious double for the last time on the day before the alley was at last reduced to rubble—it was the only time they acknowledged each other's presence. "Who was he," Félix wondered, "and what grief brought him there?" Two solitary, isolated mourners haunting a doubly doomed spot—did Félix invent this suspiciously literary tableau? If so, he was dramatizing his sorrow over the loss of a friend, his nostalgia for a disappearing Paris, and also the tragic end of a writer undervalued by his contemporaries.

Baudelaire's tribute to Nerval was brief and pointed: he wrote about the recent death of a writer of "admirable honesty" and "lofty intelligence" who "went discreetly without disturbing anyone—so discreetly that his discretion resembled contempt—to set loose his soul in the blackest street he could find." Typically provocative, Baudelaire veered from these passing remarks (slipped into the preface to some of his translations of Poe) to a defense of suicide—which, he argued, "is sometimes the most reasonable action in a life." Embracing for himself the persona of the *poète maudit*, scorned by society and at odds with the basic terms of bourgeois existence, he enlisted Nerval in his cause—posthumously.

———————— ❖ ————————

FÉLIX FIRST MET Baudelaire in the Jardin du Luxembourg, probably in the fall of 1843. Twenty-three-year-old Félix was parked on his usual shady bench with a few friends, including Banville, when a bizarre black-clad figure came straight at them down the esplanade: a young man with thick black shoulder-length curls, an oxblood cravat, pale pink gloves, and impeccably polished boots. It was Baudelaire, aged twenty-two and already renowned in bohemian circles as a versifying dandy.

The whole little group trooped off to Baudelaire's apartment on the Quai d'Anjou on the Île Saint-Louis, two rooms and a study, comfortably furnished, in the attic of the seventeenth-century Hôtel Pimodan (today known as the Hôtel de Lauzun). For Félix, this was luxury, even the cheap musk Baudelaire sprinkled on the carpets ("To tell the truth, the odor was a bit strong") and the black and red wallpaper covering both walls and ceilings.

The two young men became instant friends. "We immediately told each other everything since there was nothing to hide and all was shared in this corner of bohemia." Mutual assistance was at the heart of their friendship, favors asked and granted at any hour, day or night.

Did Félix admit right away that until several months earlier he had been the lover of Baudelaire's mistress, Jeanne Duval, a beautiful Haitian-born actress and dancer? Félix saw her on stage at the Théâtre du Panthéon and tracked her down to the apartment on the rue Saint-Georges where she lived with her maid. In his memoirs, Banville described Duval as "a colored girl, very tall, who held high her dark head, artless and superb, crowned with violently crinkled hair, and who moved like a queen, full of feral grace, at once divine and bestial." Nadar was lavish and explicit in his praise of her physical attributes, as well as her manner: "serious, proud, even a little disdainful."

Baudelaire probably knew about Félix's affair with Jeanne, or learned of it soon enough. Camaraderie among fellow bohemians was, according to Félix, intimately communal—no restraints, no secrets, as though they lived under a glass dome. When he and Baudelaire quarreled, which they did on occasion, it was never over a woman. Félix was one of the few friends Baudelaire addressed with the informal *tu*. Yet camaraderie had its limits. With the exception of Banville and Asselineau, Félix was not fond of Baudelaire's close friends. He found their interests narrow (too exclusively literary) and thought of them as sycophants worshipping Baudelaire and aping his style. One of these acolytes, Alexandre Privat d'Anglemont, a kind of professional *flâneur* who later published two collections of anecdotes about bohemian Paris, Félix dismissed as a liar. The inseparable Goncourt brothers, Edmond and Jules, he deemed self-important. For Champfleury, the pen name of Jules François Felix Fleury-Husson, an art critic and novelist, Félix's contempt was wholehearted and somewhat inexplicable. He grumbled about Champfleury's vanity, but rivalry and unflattering reviews were the actual source of the bad blood between them.

Félix claimed to prefer the unpretentious and unfussy ragtag band clustered around Murger—forgetting that Champfleury had been, briefly, one of Murger's roommates.

What did Félix see when he looked at his friend Baudelaire? The photographs tell the story. The only one that can be conclusively dated—from early 1855, shortly before the publication of some of the finest poems from *Les Fleurs du mal*—shows the poet reclined in an armchair, one pale hand tenderly by his cheek, a dreamy character caught unawares; the other hand rests on his thigh, a little cigar between two fingers, a casual bohemian touch. The pose verges on cliché, especially the faraway eyes: the poet as mystical seer. Affectionate and reverent, it's the earliest surviving Nadar photo of Baudelaire—and the only one that's in any way gentle.

Later, the expression hardens: arrogant or wary or ironic, the flat or downturned mouth always stubborn, the dark eyes glinting with defiance or anger.

In one photograph, probably from 1862, Baudelaire nearly drops his guard. Seated, velvet-collared jacket buttoned up, hands deep in pockets, head slightly tilted, he looks at the viewer with questioning eyes. Is he trying to make a connection, to appeal for understanding? Perhaps it's only the soft focus and the pallor of the face against the austere background that gives the impression of a man in search of sympathy.

Félix worried that people who didn't know his friend would find him hard-hearted, when in fact, though reticent and circumspect, he was full of compassion for human misery. Looking back in old age, Felix thought of him as "tormented by a vague need to flee from himself"—and tormenting others with his urge to achieve "singularity," to provoke and astonish, a need so insatiable that Asselineau imagined Baudelaire coming home at night and sleeping *underneath* his bed—just to surprise himself.

And what did Baudelaire think of Félix? The differences between the two friends were apparent to all: one was focused, intense, cerebral, private, the other restlessly exuberant, poking his nose into every corner, dreaming up wild schemes, avidly collecting friends. In his journals Baudelaire wrote: "Nadar is the most astonishing expression of vitality. Adrien told me that his brother had all the vital organs in double. It made me jealous to see him succeed so well in everything that wasn't abstract."

These differences weren't merely a matter of temperament. Though he disliked the term because of its military associations, Baudelaire was an avant-garde poet and a canny celebrator of what he called *modernité*. As a critic, he advanced sophisticated aesthetic ideas with a force of conviction and a rhetorical ingenuity unavailable to Félix, who could write energetically, persuasively, accurately, even charmingly, but was never at his best when discussing intangibles. He could cope, as Baudelaire noticed, with "everything that wasn't abstract." From Baudelaire's writing, one could distill a blueprint for the modern man—and that man would bear a striking resemblance to Nadar, the celebrity our Félix was on the road to becoming. Yet though he was an unabashed fan of the new, hungry for innovation and discovery, eager for progress to sweep aside the old, the term *avant-garde* doesn't suit Félix; it implies a self-consciousness about art that he mostly lacked.

MURGER WARNED THAT bohemians would end up either smothered by the embrace of the cultural establishment, in a state hospital, or in a pauper's grave. Baudelaire avoided all three of those fates, but only barely. He contracted syphilis as a young man, took too much laudanum, smoked too much opium, and drank too much brandy—his health broke down. A stroke in 1866 left him paralyzed on his right side and suffering from aphasia; the last seventeen months of his life were spent in clinics, first in Brussels and then in Paris, where he was comfortably installed in a nursing home near the place de l'Étoile, in a ground-floor room with a view of the garden and the Arc de Triomphe. Félix visited him there often and also brought Ernestine to the patient's bedside. In the early months he organized Monday-night dinners at his house for Baudelaire and a few old friends; around the table, Baudelaire made himself understood with improvised sign language. Though he seemed at first to enjoy these reunions, one day he simply refused to come, letting it be known that the dinners were too tiring and led to insomnia and depression.

Félix recorded their last conversation, which took place by the window in the nursing home. The topic was the immortality of the soul, and the talk rather one-sided, since Baudelaire could only gesture with his left hand; the two words he could form were *oh* and *crénom*, a mild expletive roughly equivalent to "for god's sake." Félix thought he could tell what his friend meant to say by reading his eyes.

"Come on, how can you believe in God?" I asked again.

Baudelaire moved away from the rail we were leaning on and gestured to the sky. Before us and above us . . . outlining the powerful silhouette of the Arc de Triomphe in fire and gold, the splendid spectacle of the setting sun.

"*Crénom! oh! crénom!*" he insisted, reproaching me, indignant, punching the sky.

He died on the morning of August 31, 1867. In a wholly admiring obituary in *Le Figaro*, Félix took pains to emphasize nonbohemian aspects of the poet's character: his fervent admiration for well-made things, his conscientiousness in work, his religious devotion to duty, and his professional dignity. Baudelaire died intestate, which meant that his mother took charge of distributing his possessions to various friends; to Félix, she gave watercolors by

Constantin Guys, the artist whom Baudelaire, in a seminal essay, had hailed as "the painter of modern life."

THERE'S A SAD and bewildering coda to the story of this long friendship. In the last two years of his life, Félix wrote a short biographical sketch called *Charles Baudelaire intime*. The puzzlement begins with the subtitle: *Le poète vierge* (The Virgin Poet). Since it's commonly accepted that Baudelaire kept mistresses (including Jeanne Duval), frequented prostitutes, and died suffering from syphilis, one assumes at first that this claim is metaphorical—that Félix is arguing for his friend's essential spiritual innocence. Not at all. He flatly asserts that the poet died a virgin, that all his life he recoiled from women. He claims that all their bohemian pals were agreed that this was the case, and that all the women they frequented (every one of them generous and welcoming) insisted that Baudelaire never approached them in any way.

But what of Jeanne Duval? Félix explains that Baudelaire's relationship with his "mistress" was platonic, that he visited her only between two and four in the afternoon, and that nothing happened during those hours to provoke the jealousy of her other lover (Félix).

The charitable explanation for this bizarre document (which was published posthumously in 1911) is that Félix was troubled by the commonly accepted idea that Baudelaire was syphilitic and promoted the myth of the Virgin Poet to preserve what he thought of as his friend's "innate chastity." He was curating his friend's reputation, as he had Nerval's. (Félix also liked to argue, and this was a cause certain to appeal to his contrarian instincts.)

He knew that he was painting an unflattering portrait, that the idea of a "virgin poet, recoiling from the female," might appear "unsympathetic, repulsive even," especially to women. He suggested that our "compassion" would keep us from turning away from an "acknowledged pathological case."

Was it really for Baudelaire's sake that Félix peddled this fantasy? His motives were possibly less than generous. He began *Charles Baudelaire intime* with the story of his own affair with

Jeanne Duval; in other words, he began by boasting (in graphic detail) of an amorous conquest—a conquest he then denied Baudelaire. He proceeded to depict the poet as a kind of misogynistic eunuch. This smacks of betrayal. It's possible that Félix, at age eighty-eight, was worried that his friend who'd died forty years earlier had grown more famous than he; it's possible that he wrote *Charles Baudelaire intime* out of jealousy, in the spirit of competition. If so, his judgment failed him.

⸻

THERE WAS NO JEALOUSY when they met, no competition. They were part of a band of brothers, all squeezed around a table upstairs at the Café Momus, pockets empty—not enough money between them to buy a drink.

For Baudelaire, as for Nerval, living like a bohemian was a choice linked to convictions about art and society. Both were adamant in their rejection of conventional bourgeois values. But both had rich relatives, and both burned through inheritances while mingling with friends like Félix whose families could offer meager financial support at best. To be broke, or worse, was the bohemian way—a badge of honor. Friends borrowed from friends, signed promissory notes, and guaranteed each other's debts. But when the music stopped, inevitably someone would be left standing. Baudelaire, Nerval, and Félix all found themselves at one time or another unable to pay their bills. Once creditors closed in, it mattered little whether it was a fortune that had been squandered or only a modest, hard-earned sum—yet it's worth noting that of the three, only Félix spent any time locked up in jail for debt. Arrested early one morning in the summer of 1850, he was incarcerated in the Clichy debtor's prison, an experience he described in an essay published in February of the following year.

Prudently signed F.-T. Molin (a pseudonym that yokes *Félix Tournachon* with *Molin,* the name of his paternal grandmother's family), "Clichy in 1850" is a typical Nadar performance, a playful guide to the amusing oddities of life in a prison that is perfectly comfortable and civilized, "charming," even—except for the high stone walls, bolted doors, and barred windows. Being under lock and key drives the imprisoned debtors slightly cuckoo, and the fun of the piece is the taxonomy of their various derangements. The madness induced by debtor's prison mostly consists of radical denial, and most of the symptoms are variations on the prisoners' shared delusion that they're all on the verge of release—just a stride from the street. One subsymptom seems tailor-made for Félix's satirical talents: the mania for moneymaking projects. An otherwise level-headed prisoner explains a scheme that will make enough to spring him in just eight days: "A *Newspaper of the Clichy prison*. There's a hundred thousand francs to be made there . . . and that's not counting the personals!"

The mood turns sober with a description of the philanthropic society established by the Clichy inmates and dedicated to ameliorating conditions for the imprisoned debtors. The essay concludes with an impassioned denunciation of the "iniquitous, and moreover useless" law that condemns debtors to jail, a punishment that demoralizes and dishonors them yet does nothing to repay the debt.

At the very end, a twist: Félix announces that thanks to the aid of "a devoted businessman and a skillful lawyer," he himself was released from Clichy just as soon as he wanted to leave. In other words, he claims he spent more than a month locked up in a cell because he wasn't yet ready to go. Earlier on in the essay, a fellow inmate sees him taking notes and tells him, "If you publish anything about Clichy, make sure to make it gay. The creditors must be made to believe that we're much amused here. It disgusts them." The note taking establishes the possibility that his stint behind bars was a kind of participatory journalism—and if he was merely collecting material, then none of the stigma, none of the humiliation of debtor's prison, clings to him.

But there's another way to read this twist: his belief that he could have walked out of jail at any time is actually a manifestation of the mania he's just described—a delusion like that of every other debtor. And indeed, the publisher Jules Hetzel, a friend and benefactor, wrote to Félix at Clichy to say that no, he would *not* provide five hundred francs to free him. Our hero had clearly been scrounging for money to satisfy his creditor, looking for the generous patron and clever lawyer who could spring him from prison.

His halfhearted and ironic attempt to wash away the stain of Clichy by implying that he'd been gathering good material rather than merely languishing in jail perhaps suggests that at age thirty he was tiring of his hand-to-mouth existence, growing ambivalent about bohemia, or just plain growing up. A nomadic decade had ended with a term in debtor's prison—better than the morgue or the state hospital, but as far removed as ever from the kind of success that spells security.

IV

THE WRITING LIFE

O N THE PRINTED INVITATION TO HIS *FÊTE CHAMPÊTRE,* Félix identified the vicomte de la Tour Nadard as an *homme de lettres* (man of letters), an eighteenth-century term used to describe an occupation that became viable as a profession only in the nineteenth century. In the decades since the Revolution, when the legal rights of French authors were codified for the first time, a new literary world had emerged, a market for the written word exploited by a new class of literary professionals. A rapidly expanding readership was courted by a broad array of newspapers, magazines, journals, and gazettes, some lavish, some cheaply printed, some narrowly targeted, some widely distributed—in all, a sudden flood of newsprint. Paris was already crowded with scribblers trying to make a living with their pen by the time the Société des gens de lettres was founded in 1838. (Some of the scribblers were women, hence *gens:* "The Society of *People* of Letters.") Inspired by Honoré de Balzac, the organization was expressly devoted to promoting the interests of authors and protecting their rights. Among the earliest and most active members were Dumas, George Sand, and Victor Hugo, three writers with whom Félix would have extensive dealings. In his early twenties, Félix's most pressing desire was to establish himself as a writer, and in 1844 he proudly joined the Société des gens de lettres. The *société* became an important part of his life: he relied on it for help when his work was pirated by unscrupulous provincial newspapers; he appealed to it for funds when he was broke; and he published stories in the *Bulletin de la Société des gens de lettres*. True to form, he used the *société* to widen the circle of his acquaintances: he would later work with, sketch, and photograph many of the writers, editors, and publishers he met at the general assemblies.

Homme de lettres was a new profession, as was the kind of writing done by Félix and his fellow journalists. Over the course of the nineteenth century, newspapers gave more and more space to gossip, fashion, and theater and art reviews. Literary doodling of all sorts, including fiction, found its way into otherwise staid publications—periodicals hitherto austerely devoted to foreign and domestic news, ideas, and politics. A new word, *feuilleton*, was coined: at first it meant the bottom of the page—where articles about cultural matters would appear—and later the article itself.

The audience for this kind of journalism hadn't existed until recently, and nobody knew how long the enthusiasm of the new readers would last. A feuilleton written for a freshly hatched newspaper was even more ephemeral than most writing: the words might be forgotten almost at once, the paper itself could vanish a week later, and the whole fad might pass within a year. The fleeting, insecure aspect of the entire enterprise has a modern feel, while the hankering after self-expression (a surprising share of early feuilletons are written in the first person) seems a late flowering of the Romantic impulse.

The second article Félix ever published, which appeared in a Lyon weekly called *Fanal du commerce* on August 3, 1838, just a few weeks after he'd returned to Paris, was called *Mon premier feuilleton* (My First Column). It begins as a satirical self-portrait of the author as fledgling *feuilletonist:* "I was a sight to behold, walking with my head held high, as though everyone could read on my forehead the title *homme de lettres*—Homme de lettres! how good that name sounded to my ears! If I had dared I would have shouted it out in the streets." Cynical and self-aware—and surely hoping to sound sophisticated—he declares vanity (*amour-propre*) to be a writer's principal motivation. "*Amour-propre* is a tyrant each of us must submit to," he writes, "an imperious tyrant that always requires fresh caresses and fresh flattery; and what can deliver more intense satisfaction, always renewed, than publicity?" He was being facetious and also honest: at the age of eighteen, he was already hooked on the thrill of seeing his name in print.

Satire, sometimes veiled, sometimes brazen, was everywhere in the pages of the small press, which was in de facto opposition to the established press and which often adopted a subversive tone, politically and socially. The idea was to make sly fun of the bourgeoisie without alienating the bourgeois reader, and to make sly fun of the government without rousing the censors. And yet paradoxically, these little newspapers and magazines were instruments of upward mobility. This was how a young bohemian, a writer or illustrator, could make his mark, get noticed, and achieve respectability— respectability of the very sort he might be busy mocking. It was not unheard of for an editor at a fledgling journal to crave a career in politics; some even stepped nimbly, in those topsy-turvy times, from opposition to government.

Félix was always ambitious, and not only for his art—a trait that set him apart from most bohemians. He wanted to be caressed and flattered by publicity, to taste fame and fortune. Even as a teenager, he longed to be the driving force in grand projects. In the year before he announced his social ambitions with his party at the Élysée Nadard, he made his professional and commercial ambitions apparent by joining two start-up newspapers, one financial, the other legal, and co-founding (at age nineteen) a magazine aimed squarely at the rich and wellborn.

The two newspapers, *Le Négociateur* and *L'Audience*, were conceived and bankrolled by Polydore Millaud, whose spectacular career in publishing and finance earned him the nickname "Millaud-Million." Self-taught and self-made, the son of an unprosperous Jewish ribbon merchant in Bordeaux, Millaud was a mere seven years older than Félix. One of his early successes was *Le Gamin de Paris*, a weekly paper established in 1836 and sold exclusively at theater doors, a novel idea at the time. It was probably through theater journalism that Félix and Millaud came into contact, but at *Le Négociateur*, devoted to the concerns of finance and industry, Félix worked as little more than a dogsbody. Within a matter of months, Millaud had founded *L'Audience*, which covered court hearings and trials, dryly at first but with a growing appetite for the sensational. Félix was named editor. Soon the paper was reporting the news with dramatic flair and also running fictional accounts of grotesque and macabre crimes of the sort being prosecuted in Paris courtrooms. Bataille tells us that Millaud would appear at the offices of *L'Audience*, rub his hands, and tell his young staff, "Give it *zip*, my sons! Give it zip."

Millaud later made and lost a fortune (not for the first time) founding *Le Petit Journal*, the most widely read French paper of the nineteenth century. He was a mentor to Félix as well as an inspiration: he gave him both a job and a close-up view of what fresh ideas, gumption, and publicity could achieve. And when the opportunity came to put that lesson to the test, Félix grabbed it. In July 1839, one of his Quartier Latin friends, Alfred Francey, inherited six thousand francs. Félix and his pal Léon-Noël knew exactly how this windfall should be spent. Within months, the three young men had launched a lavishly produced illustrated literary magazine called *Le Livre d'or, keepsake du grand monde*. The name spells out the concept: a high society keepsake, it was supposed to be the opposite of ephemeral. Its founders predicted that *Le Livre d'or* would be "the book of the nobility . . . each patrician would see in its brilliance a reflection of his person." They assured their posh public (or perhaps themselves) that their magazine would become "the indispensable ornament in salons and boudoirs." At the very least they hoped to attract subscribers capable of appreciating the "luxury, elegance, good taste and variety" of each issue—for a mere thirty-six francs per annum.

The bluster, flattery, and overstated snobbery of these pronouncements can be partly forgiven in the light of a genuinely impressive list of "collaborators," among them Balzac, Dumas, Alfred de Vigny, Théophile Gautier, and Gérard de Nerval. That such prestigious figures were willing to lend their names to the newborn venture testifies to the powers of persuasion of the three young men behind it and also to the fluidity of the literary scene. Even established writers were eager to try out new venues. Who knew which newfangled scheme would succeed?

Francey and Léon-Noël ran the business side of the operation, while Félix was editor in chief. The first two issues, printed on vellum paper, featured a charming, somewhat soppy ghost story by Gautier and little else of note, though each page was surrounded by an elaborate border, and the first paragraph of each contribution was decorated with a historiated initial, as though it were an illuminated manuscript. Promised for future issues was a short novel by Balzac, *La Frélore*. This was not an empty promise: the manuscript was bought and paid for. But *Le Livre d'or* went bust before the first installment of *La Frélore* saw print.

It was Félix who went to fetch the proofs of the novel from Balzac, an exciting encounter for a budding journalist with a weakness for celebrity. Years later he recalled his visit to the rue Richelieu, the fifth-floor apartment draped in violet fabric, and the dramatic gesture of spilling five hundred francs across the table for the famous author—whose imposing girth was wrapped in what looked like a brown monk's robe. Félix spruced up the anecdote with a suspiciously apt line of dialogue: when the youngster arrived, he tentatively offered to bargain down the price, whereupon the great man pronounced magnificently, "Sir, you can't have it both ways, you are here to deal either with a merchant selling cotton bonnets or with an illustrious writer." Mortification for Félix.

Announced as a weekly, *Le Livre d'or* survived for about a month, from mid-September to mid-October 1839; only three issues were distributed. Yet its demise did nothing to dampen the enthusiasm of our young entrepreneur. He went back to work for Millaud, but switched (sometime before September 1841) to an opposition newspaper, *Le Commerce,* whose editor in chief, Charles de Lesseps, was a moderate republican for whom Félix developed a sincere and lasting admiration. Lesseps put Félix to work on a primitive version of a wire service: during the morning, Félix and his colleagues would rush around town gathering all kinds of news, political, financial, cultural; in the afternoon, whatever items they'd collected were stitched into a single column and sent out by mail for publication the following day in the regional editions of the newspaper. Though hardly the literary glory Félix dreamed of, this steady job gave him a foothold at a publication very much in the public eye. He developed an enduring fascination with the latest news; even as an old man, he had to have his daily fix of current events and political gossip.

It was in the pages of *Le Commerce,* in November 1843, that Félix's first truly successful feuilleton made its debut. "La mort de Dupuytren," which was reprinted many times in both Parisian and provincial papers, is a clever mix of fact and fiction that gives a pleasing dramatic shape to the death of Baron Guillaume Dupuytren, the most famous French surgeon of the nineteenth century. (His fame rested in part on having treated Napoléon's hemorrhoids.) Félix's story pits the notoriously inflexible Dupuytren, a medical pioneer wedded to positivist principles and allergic to superstition, against a simple country priest who has walked to the capital at the behest of his devoted parishioners to ask the great doctor to operate on a life-threatening abscess. The priest's stoicism and steady, patient kindness break through Dupuytren's icy contempt. The surgeon agrees to operate and saves the priest's life; in return, when Dupuytren falls mortally ill several years later, the priest provides spiritual comfort—in effect, he saves the surgeon's soul.

In a postscript, Félix disavowed any dogmatic intent, claiming that he was merely retelling a story he'd heard—because it was a true story about a great man. This unconvincing disclaimer only draws attention to the moral of the tale. By showing the beneficent influence of a saintly cleric on a celebrated man of science, by exposing the fallacy of Dupuytren's profound disdain for "human things," Félix is suggesting that the sharp blade of scientific advancement should be guided by moral concerns, and that progress ought to serve both the material interests of the people and high ideals—a characteristic combination of the practical and the visionary.

Heavy-handed endings, not necessarily happy but freighted with poetic justice, are a constant feature of Félix's writing. One of the fixed opinions he formed over the course of endless debates held in cafés and on the park benches of the Luxembourg was that fiction had to be moral—it had to promote a greater good. Though he revered Balzac, for example, he faulted him for an absence of uplift and for the inappropriate distribution of punishments and rewards. Friends and colleagues noted the discrepancy between Félix's immoderate bohemian behavior and his straitlaced fictions. One of them joked, "One hoped for scandal from Nadar's inkwell, but only pure virtue came out of it. Nadar thus struck a blow at his own reputation."

The warm reception of "La mort de Dupuytren" encouraged Félix to finish a novel he'd been working on in fits and starts for so long that his slow progress had become the subject of jibes from his fellow bohemians. The delay may have been compounded by the work he took on as a secretary to a rich industrialist, Victor Grandin, who was a delegate (*député*) in the Chamber of Deputies. A member of the opposition when he hired Félix but later, during the Second Republic, a monarchist, Grandin distinguished himself by fervently opposing a law limiting child labor. No less an authority than Karl Marx referred to Grandin as "the most fanatical instrument of bourgeois reaction." How could Félix have been willing to associate himself, even for a few months, with a politician who espoused views that must have been repugnant to him? Possibly he convinced himself that he was gathering useful material: one of the characters in his novel is a rich man who wants to get elected to the Chamber of Deputies.

Published serially in *Le Commerce* (the first of thirty-five installments appeared in December 1843, the last in May 1844), *La Robe de Déjanire* was Félix's first novel—and also his last. A mash-up of Balzacian realism, sentimental melodrama, and utopian socialist propaganda, it contains moments of genuine excitement and many passages of witty, incisive prose—but too often strikes an oppressively moral note.

In the hallowed tradition of a young person writing a first novel, Félix wrote about what he knew. *La Robe* follows the fortunes of a quartet of penniless lads living, when we meet them, in a garret. All are educated, talented, and broke—and there the similarities end. There's a jolly, good-hearted painter dedicated to his art; a craven and ineffectual poet; a cynical aristocrat determined to claw his way back into high society; and a charming, dreamy young man who's dabbled in this and that (engineering, law, medicine, painting, and literature) and has accomplished exactly nothing. As always in Félix's fiction, character is destiny; each eventually receives his just deserts.

The villain of the piece, the déclassé aristocrat Félix Beauplaisir de Simons, whose friends mockingly call him le Marquis, has decided that he will marry money: "It's through women that one succeeds," he declares. He achieves his aim with cruel efficiency and for a short while lives his dream, rich and respected, frequenting the best Parisian society. But his crimes are exposed, and he's disgraced and "excluded from all honorable salons." He travels abroad, indulges in "sad and shameful passions," and dies young, "worn out by excess."

Meanwhile the dreamy, irresolute young Claudien Forget embarks on a passionate love affair with a banker's wife. After he and his lover run away to Brussels, they gradually sink into abject poverty, a downward spiral from which neither recovers. Passionate and well-intentioned but spineless and lazy, Claudien is the soft side of bohemia, a reminder to the reader (and the author) of the grim fate that awaits impoverished young men with no appetite for hard work. Claudien isn't a villain but rather a victim—a victim of his own weakness and the corrupting influence of idleness and illicit passion.

The hero is Claudien's bastard brother, Louis Armand, a self-taught working man who improbably combines capacious intelligence, utter moral rectitude, charisma, and "large and generous" socialist principles—principles that work in practice! The name of this paragon is made up of the first names of two men Félix greatly admired, the historian and socialist philosopher Louis Blanc, and Armand Barbès, a firebrand revolutionary. Impossibly virtuous and always on hand to save the day, Louis Armand is eventually elected to the national legislature and becomes a pillar of the republican opposition. The novel's pious concluding remarks are his: "A salary is owed only to action. A dream is not a fact, any more than emotions are principles."

Villain, victim, hero—all three are aspects of the authorial ego projected onto the page. Félix Beauplaisir de Simons shares a first name with the author and a similarly strong determination to succeed. Le marquis de Beauplaisir is surely related to le vicomte de la Tour Nadard, but only distantly: Beauplaisir's brand of ambition is "cold and ignoble"—and no one ever accused Nadar of being cold. Charmingly scattered and passionate (like Claudien), Félix believed as fervently as Armand in social ownership and cooperative enterprises. For Félix, writing the novel must have been like telling his own fortune: which of his character traits would predominate, and how would they shape his fate?

On the evidence of *La Robe de Déjanire*, a career as a novelist was not in the cards. The first third of the book, with the backdrop of a shabby Paris neighborhood and the four young bohemians crowded into their attic room, is lively and evocative. But the plot, as it cranks up, proves weak: surprising dramatic events, generally sparked by coincidence, are followed by clumsy flashbacks: *We must explain, before going any further, how it came to be that X found himself face to face with Y.*

Several fraudulent financial schemes are described with authority and evident relish—but these are among the rare occasions when Félix allows vice to show its dark appeal. The novel's most dispiriting passages are devoted to a strident disquisition on the perils of hiding away with a lover. Living in sin was clearly something Félix knew all about—just as he knew all about going hungry in a leaky, drafty garret. A page and a half on the pathology of prolonged and unrelieved intimacy ends with this grim

judgment on the false bliss of adulterous couples: "solitary plea-
sures, egotistical contentment that diminishes and enervates, that
degrades and kills."

On the page, at least, Claudien and his married lover remain
fully clothed—the most they're allowed is an ardent embrace.
(Even so, she bears his child.) Félix was hardly a prude, but his
convictions about the morality of fiction—which prevented him
from reading Flaubert's *Madame Bovary* when it was published
a dozen years later—made him unwilling to describe any part of
the female anatomy other than the face: this despite his sharp eye
for the human form. Several long passages itemize and analyze in
minute detail the facial features of relatively minor characters, and
in one case he invokes the theories of Johann Kaspar Lavater and
Franz Josef Gall, leading exponents of physiognomy and phrenol-
ogy, both of whom were convinced that a person's moral and intel-
lectual nature was reflected in his or her external appearance—a
long forehead indicating intelligence, for example, or a short one
volatility. Félix's fascination with faces would become even more
pronounced a few years later.

La Robe is the work of a young man with his eyes open wide, ac-
tively, enthusiastically engaged with the life around him, and trying to determine the best path to follow. (The painter roommate,
after some modest success, allows that he's "on the right path—to
the right path.") But at the age of twenty-four, Félix lacked the skill
to knit together a first-rate novel. What success *La Robe* achieved
came from its serial publication: it ran in *L'Audience* as well as *Le
Commerce* and later in two other small-circulation papers. Published in book form in 1844, in a three-volume edition, it failed to
make a mark.

He took the hint: it would be nearly twenty years before he set
out to write another full-length book. Instead, he scaled back his
ambition and settled for writing short pieces tailored for periodicals where he had established connections. What books he did publish were compilations of feuilletons he'd sold here and there. This
pragmatic approach to literary matters stemmed from necessity: he
needed to earn a living. He had no time for the vagaries of inspiration and little patience for art for art's sake, the slogan of his friend

Gautier. In his youth, Félix wrote with difficulty; five years after *La Robe* he remarked in a letter to a stranger, "It's never for my pleasure that I bring myself to write, even if it's just two lines."

After he stopped trying to earn a living by writing, he no longer found it difficult to write. In his thirties he produced a considerable quantity of art criticism, often accompanied by caricatures of the paintings in question. In middle age he wrote out of passionate conviction about human flight, and later in life he did write for pleasure—and because he couldn't seem to stop himself. Writing was one of the constants in his turbulent, whirlwind life.

And yet had he continued as a journalist, had writing remained his sole or principal occupation, Nadar would very likely be forgotten today. When he put down his pen and put aside the dream of becoming a respected *homme de lettres,* and instead picked up a draughtman's pencil, he started along the path to the path that led to lasting fame.

V

"All Is Lost! Nadar Has Learned to Draw!"

A N AMUSINGLY SCABROUS LITTLE BOOK APPEARED IN early 1844, made up of snippets of gossip—some malicious, some salacious—about the theater world of Paris. The promiscuity of young actresses and their greed for money featured prominently in its pages, as did the foolish lust of the men, mostly married, who pursued them. A clutch of writers contributed anonymously to the book, among them Baudelaire and his pal Privat d'Anglemont. It was called *Mystères galans des théâtres de Paris* (Saucy Mysteries of the Paris Theater), and on its cover was a drawing of a devil's head with tiny actors performing on the top of his conveniently flattened skull and also in his gaping mouth. A jaunty little *N* below the devil's chin gives one hint as to the artist's identity; another is the tuft of random hair sprouting from the devil's cheek: in Nadar's youth, unruly facial hair sprouted from moles on his cheeks.

Did Félix supply this illustration because he couldn't quite bring himself to make a written contribution to a scabrous book? (There's not an ounce of moral uplift in the entire volume.) Did he decide to draw a devil so as to advertise the naughtiness within? And is that tuft of hair his way of admitting that by supplying the cover illustration he had succumbed to a devilish temptation? Who could blame him: it would have been hard not to take part in a project that so many of his fellow bohemians were evidently having fun with.

It's not clear when Félix began to draw, or when he decided that scratching out illustrations might add significantly to his income.

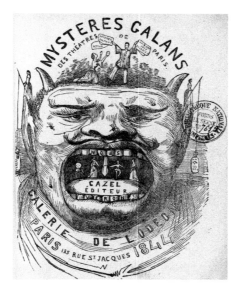

It's possible that the return to Paris, in about 1845, of his mother and younger brother added to his sense that he had to make money by any means, so as to contribute to their support. Adrien hoped to become a painter and eventually enrolled, with Félix's help, in the École des Beaux-Arts. In the meantime, through his many contacts in the press, Félix found work for Adrien as an illustrator for magazines and newspapers. This was probably the moment when the older brother saw the opportunity to expand the range of his own activities. Caricature would gradually replace writing as the engine of his career; within a decade, it would make him famous and the name Nadar a byword for wit and invention.

The transformation from writer to artist was a slow process, barely perceptible at first. Félix placed a few of his drawings here and there in publications where his journalism also appeared. Only in the summer of 1847 did he receive his first major commission. A friend who had founded a weekly called *Journal du dimanche* asked him to produce a series of portraits of people from the literary world, each sketch accompanied by written remarks—in sum, a *Galerie des gens de lettres*. The scope of the plan was impressive: the *galerie* was to include a hundred writers and journalists. But the paper folded after fifty-nine of the portraits had appeared, in three installments. When it disappeared in late August 1847, Félix must have experienced a powerful sense of déjà vu: *Journal du dimanche* had been in existence less than a year.

Most of the sketches were of fellow members of the Société des gens de lettres, though all kinds of scribblers were represented, from the very famous (Hugo, Balzac, Dumas) to the utterly unknown. The drawings were caricatures, what the French sometimes call *portraits-charge*, which hearkens back to the derivation of the word, the Italian *caricare*—"to charge or load." A caricature is a charged portrait in the sense that the exaggeration of certain features is meant to intensify the resemblance—and, ideally, reveal some truth about the subject. The method Félix adopted was to draw a big head on a little body, a technique popularized by Honoré Daumier, among others. The caricatures in the *galerie* are apprentice work, the quality very uneven. Some of the drawings are crude and awkward, others fussy and unconvincing; only a few show signs of real promise.

The drawings are embedded in a rambling text that begins anew with each weekly installment as a letter to the editor in chief, then segues into prose sketches of the week's writers.

Facetious, full of winks and nudges, and nearly devoid of biographical information, the text is comically obsessive about reputation and how to qualify and quantify it. Not much of the commentary is friendly, and even the admiring passages are usually accompanied by caustic jabs. His sketch of Balzac, for instance, begins with a put-down:

> Women of thirty—who are actually forty—who hoped to find in their admiring propagandist a young man with an agreeable physique, will probably refuse absolutely to recognize the fat fellow we're presenting to them.

After praising Balzac's genius ("so impulsive, so varied, so infinite"), Félix trotted out the grand pronouncement that ended his attempt, years earlier, to negotiate with the author ("you are here to deal either with a merchant selling cotton bonnets or with an illustrious writer")—evidence, according to Félix, of "pride pushed to the point of folly." Félix had evidently come to the conclusion that

abrasive commentary would attract the kind of notice a fledgling caricaturist requires.

What's interesting about the *galerie* isn't the writing or the draftsmanship (neither shows him at his best) but rather the ambition behind the project and Félix's intensely social methods, his urge to work with and through and on the people around him, to note all the links between writers and editors and critics. He saw the literary world as a web and placed himself at or near the center, emphasizing his personal ties to many of the fifty-nine writers. The *galerie* marks the beginning of his career as a curator of celebrities and would-be celebrities.

Six months later he felt ready to submit a caricature to the most influential of the illustrated journals: *Le Charivari*, a daily founded in 1832 by Charles Philipon, who would become a hugely important figure in Félix's life—a demanding, inspiring boss, a stern mentor, a friend, a father figure. Félix later wrote, "Philipon personified, I almost said created, political caricature." His most famous gag was to use his pen to transform the jowly king Louis-Philippe I into a pear—whereupon the pear became a symbol for the regime, universal shorthand for satirists. Balzac, who in 1830 helped Philipon found the satirical weekly *La Caricature* (where the pear first saw print), called him "Duke of Lithograph, Marquis of Drawing, Count of Woodcut, Baron Burlesque, Sir Caricature." Of the scores of talented artists who worked closely with him over the course of a career that spanned several decades and successive regimes, Daumier and Gustave Doré were the most famous, Félix perhaps the most grateful.

Their long and constructive collaboration might have had its start at the very beginning of 1848, but was delayed for many months by a sudden political upheaval, the February Revolution, which for the briefest of moments looked as though it might usher in the sort of democratic socialist government Félix dreamed of. The political situation in France had been stable, though hardly secure, since the ascension of Louis-Philippe in 1830, but in February, in just two hectic days, the government was toppled and the king fled into exile. Barricades went up all over Paris, and exuberant citizens rushed to ensure that the monarchy was indeed dead, a republic about to be born.

Where was Félix? Nobody knows. In bed with a mistress? Under a bed with the jitters? Unlike Baudelaire, he did not take to the barricades. In a kind of mea culpa composed decades later, he suggested that he had slumbered through the revolution: "In this life we lived as bohemians, day to day, aimless, idle or in sterile agitation, appallingly careless . . . in this life that never stopped, day or night, there was never, not even for a second, room to reflect.

According to my birth certificate I was some twenty-eight years old . . . in truth I was sixteen at most, maybe not even that. . . . February woke me up."

If indeed he thought of himself as harmless and hopelessly immature, the police had a different idea. They had been keeping a file on Félix Tournachon since the summer of 1842, while he was still working at *Le Commerce;* the early reports identified him as a "frenzied republican" and asserted that he engaged in rioting. The following year he was labeled a "dangerous" character for sowing subversive thoughts in the minds of impressionable university students in the Quartier Latin. That year's report ended ominously: "We're watching him closely." And then nothing for the next sixteen years! Either the files are lost, or the police lost interest.

On the evidence of *La Robe de Déjanire,* in the mid-1840s he was still a republican, possibly even frenzied: the novel's saintly hero, a proselytizing socialist, is both a man of the people and a man of action. But it's possible that at this point, brave talk from a fictional character was all Félix had the stomach for, and that when the February Revolution erupted, he was too surprised and too unsure of the outcome to take part.

He made up for his absence almost immediately by staging a pantomime that opened at the Théâtre des Funambules in mid-March. *Pierrot Ministre* was a stylized reenactment of the stirring February days, at once a political homage to the victory of the people ("the people who suffer and avenge themselves, the people strong and protective of their liberties") and a satire mocking a defeated regime. The show was a critical and commercial success, every performance sold out and the audience raucously appreciative. Félix had again bravely proclaimed his principles through art. (Pantomime, after all, is posturing taken to an extreme.) But soon enough he would have a chance to prove his commitment to a cause with deeds rather than words and images.

Pierrot Ministre was given an acid review by Félix's jealous rival, Champfleury, whose own pantomime had graced the stage of the Funambules until *Pierrot* supplanted it. Félix retaliated with a caustic, insulting article—and the outraged Champfleury challenged him to a duel, sending his seconds, Baudelaire and a journalist named Charles Toubin, to demand satisfaction. This was standard practice in bohemian circles—Félix himself had once challenged the editor of *La Silhouette* to a duel over a disparaging item that appeared in the paper; though "satisfaction" was obtained, there were no casualties and no hard feelings. On this occasion, the danger of bloodshed was averted when Félix wrote to Toubin saying that he was not available to fight because he was on his way to Poland to liberate the country from the yoke of Russian oppression, that he would be happy to give satisfaction to Champfleury immediately upon his return.

Félix and Adrien and their friend Antoine Fauchery had joined two hundred French volunteers and three hundred Polish refugees who planned to march seven hundred miles, evict the foreign occupiers (not only the Russians but also the Prussians and the Austrians), and bestow freedom on the long-suffering Poles. To call this adventure quixotic hardly does justice to the deluded folly of the ragtag expeditionary force that set off from the gates of the city at four in the morning on March 30, 1848.

Here was another form of expiation: self-imposed penance for having missed the fighting in February. But it was also the policy of the provisional government established after Louis-Philippe fled. The minister of foreign affairs, the poet Alphonse de Lamartine, spoke eloquently of the importance of Polish independence—he declared it a cause essential to France itself—and for years it had been a popular romantic enthusiasm among the students of the Quartier Latin. For Félix, there was also a personal angle: one of his closest friends was a kind, gentle, generous soul called Karol d'Anelle whose mother was Polish and who was himself a passionate Polish patriot. Félix had been listening for nearly a decade to Karol's laments over his mother's martyred country.

Almost any romantic ideal, any sacred cause, would have sufficed. In a series of letters to his mother and a few close friends, Félix made it absolutely clear that he craved a purpose, something greater than himself, and that the business of cleansing his soul was an important part of the expedition. "For my part," he wrote, "putting aside my sympathy for the Polish nation, I'm marching less for her than for the Idea that Poland represents." He was championing freedom and democracy, obeying the rousing chorus of the *Marseillaise:* "To arms, citizens/ Form your battalions/ Let's march, let's march!" In consecrating himself to a noble cause, he was also hoping for regeneration. To Asselineau, he wrote that by throwing himself headlong and wholeheartedly into danger, he experienced "the greatest happiness in the world: that of finding again the enthusiasm one had thought forever lost, gone with one's first youth." He felt revivified by his decision to join the volunteers. "I have at last found the chance to purify myself and to atone for my past life, for its frivolity and culpable thoughtlessness, by devoting myself to a larger idea."

"If I come back," he wrote, "I will come back truly a man."

Félix seems to have sincerely believed that he was marching into battle. "It's quite difficult," he wrote to Charles de Lesseps, "to get oneself killed usefully." To his mother, he wrote elaborate reassurances that suggest he himself was not at all reassured. He told Asselineau, "I will die if not without regrets and minor remorse, then at least confident and at peace"; and he admitted that writing to say good-bye ("adieu once more, adieu and adieu") brought tears to his eyes.

The whole episode could have been lifted from a Stendhal novel.

In the real world, there was never any chance that five hundred ill-equipped volunteers would succeed in freeing the Poles, but the scope of the failure (they never reached their destination, not a shot was fired, and Poland remained as oppressed as ever by foreign occupation) would perhaps have dented the idealism of a person less reflexively optimistic than Félix. After marching across France and arriving in Strasbourg on April 19, a few days behind schedule, they paused, then pushed on into Germany. Their progress was abruptly halted in Magdeburg, on the banks of the Elbe, about 150 miles from the Polish border. They were arrested, stripped of their arms, and briefly interned. A few weeks later Félix was issued a travel permit, in German, under the name Turnaczewski, and sent back to Paris by train. He arrived on June 1, two months after he'd left. Despite all his high-minded resolutions, the first order of business was to install himself at the Café de l'Europe, regale a crowd of friends with the story of his exploits, and show off his new headgear: a fur *czapka* with bright red ear flaps.

To his dismay, the fledgling Second Republic had reversed its policy of sponsoring foreign revolution—it had withdrawn support for precisely the kind of mission he'd just embraced. In April a moderate government had been elected, and popular discontent, especially among radical workers, was simmering; in late June it boiled over, and again Paris was convulsed by rebellion, which was brutally repressed, this time by a democratically elected government. Again, Félix was not involved—or if he was, he remained uncharacteristically silent about it.

Though embittered by Lamartine's about-face on the issue of Polish independence, Félix nonetheless offered his services to another official in the foreign ministry, Pierre-Jules Hetzel, a writer, editor, and publisher whose brief career in government coincided with the first nine months of the Second Republic. Hetzel sent Félix on a seemingly pointless "secret mission" to Prussia to assess the likelihood of a rumored Russian invasion; it's possible that Hetzel was trying to protect him by keeping him away from Paris at a politically precarious moment. During July and August, Félix the spy traveled under the assumed name Frédéric Haak, pretending to be a painter. Passing through Cologne, Berlin, Stettin (Szczecin), Danzig (Gdańsk), Königsberg, and Tilsit (Sovetsk), staying in comfortable hotels, he kept his eyes peeled for signs of war. There were none.

Back from Prussia, he landed a job at *Le Journal*, a progovernment, antisocialist newspaper founded by novelist Alphonse Karr (which survived just three months). In his memoirs, Karr gave Gérard de Nerval credit for bringing Félix to the paper's offices—and for keeping him in line while he was there. According to Karr, Félix repeatedly tried to slip into the pages of the paper remarks hostile to Lamartine, phrases Nerval and Karr carefully excised before the daily copy went to press. But Karr couldn't help liking his mischievous employee. He called Félix "an excellent fellow . . . witty, honest, and very devoted to his friends"—though he took a dim view of his "violently anarchic" political opinions.

In the beginning of September, before his brief stint at *Le Journal*, Félix had written to Hetzel saying, "I was at your service *over there;* I'm at your service here. Do you need me?" The formula worked wonders: in November Félix helped Hetzel launch a new weekly,

La Revue comique à l'usage des gens sérieux (The Comic Review for Serious People), conceived as a weapon in the battle to block the ascension of Prince Louis-Napoléon Bonaparte (nephew of Napoléon I), who had presented himself as a candidate in the presidential elections scheduled for December. Thirty-seven issues of the paper were published over a ten-month period, and in those issues Félix's signature—his distinctive *N*, with a flourish before and after—appears more than 350 times. (On the contributors page, Félix was listed among the other illustrators as "Nadard," with the terminal *d*.)

His contributions to *La Revue comique* chart his rapid evolution as a political caricaturist: in less than a year he had progressed from amateur to professional. In the paper's second issue he inaugurated a series called *Les Aventures illustrées (et non illustres) du prince pour rire* (The Illustrated [but Not Illustrious] Adventures of the Prince for a Laugh), in which he satirized Louis-Napoléon's career from cradle to candidacy, stressing at every opportunity the puniness of the pretend prince in comparison with his uncle the emperor. When for the first time Louis-Napoléon dons his uncle's iconic boots and hat—inevitably too big for him and nearly always on view, nagging reminders of his inferiority—the prince fails to recognize his own shadow: it gives him a fright.

CHAPITRE III.

SES EXPEDITIONS.

S'étant revêtu pour la première fois du costume historique, il ne se reconnaît pas dans son ombre, et il a peur!...

Next Félix dreamed up a competition to draw the portrait of Louis-Napoléon—a competition he himself judged and in which he alone competed. A clever and effective piece of mockery, his *Grand concours ouvert pour le portrait du prince pour rire* (Grand Open Competition for the Portrait of the Prince for a Laugh) consists of eighteen portraits and "preparatory sketches"; the captions, purporting to be the sardonic comments of the jury, make fun of Louis-Napoléon and also of Félix's own indifferent draftsmanship. It's a curiously postmodern performance, explicitly inviting the viewer to judge the caricaturist's art alongside the political candidate. The caption under the last portrait, which shows Louis-Napoléon as a smug, supercilious dandy, reads: "Grand Prize!!! The resemblance is striking. The fine appearance and gracious manners of the model are well rendered. The execution is perhaps a little too neat and tidy: the prince seems to have a lightning rod up his back."

The most famous of his inventions for *La Revue comique* is the eponymous antihero of a ten-part series called *La Vie publique et privée de mossieu Réac* (The Public and Private Life of Mister Réac), a crudely drawn character who represents all the shameless opportunism and small-minded self-interest of right-wing reactionaries caught up in the shifting political currents of 1848. Réac's head is always a big-nosed, big-eared outline, without shading or contour—he is literally empty-headed and flat, two-dimensional—a visual gag that made the character memorable and meaningful (he's *inhumanly* reactionary), without stretching Félix's limited talent as a draughtsman. The drawing was crude, and that became, as it often did, part of the joke. In one eight-panel sequence called *Nouvelles télégraphiques* (Telegraphic News), Réac is further flattened: transformed into a jumping jack and mounted on a relay station of the optical telegraph, the semaphore system erected in Paris at the end of the eighteenth century.

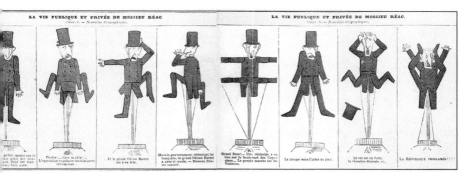

The arrangement of his paper-puppet limbs signals Réac's responses to the fast-paced events of the February Revolution; the last two panels show him seized by hair-raising panic at the flight of the king and so aghast at the proclamation of the Second Republic that his legs flip up behind his ears.

Félix's politics were too hazy and romantic to label with any precision, but certain broad outlines are worth noting. The naïve nineteen-year-old who tried to curry favor with high society in order to sell subscriptions to *Le Livre d'or, keepsake du grand monde* had become an ardent proponent of a *république démocratique et sociale* (democratic and socialist republic) or in shorthand, *démocsoc*. The opportunistic twenty-four-year-old who had signed on as secretary to a reactionary delegate in the Chamber of Deputies was now, in his late twenties, in permanent revolt against the government, even if the government was democratically elected. "I admit," he once wrote, "that it's in my nature to be always in opposition, whatever the regime that governs us—and even more, alas . . . the day when we're governed by the regime of my choice." He was a *rouge* (royalists were *blanc*) and, generally speaking, a radical *rouge*. Anything but scientific, his ideas about how society should be organized were informed by righteous enthusiasm for reform and ferocious indignation at the status quo. Friendship was also part of the equation. Félix felt about his political allies the way he did about his fellow bohemians—and the two circles overlapped, notably in the person of Baudelaire. When in late 1849 Félix traveled to London for the first time, he spent most of his few weeks there visiting friends, many of them associated with the Comité démocratique socialiste, who had been forced into exile as a result of their political activities.

The essence of his politics—both the righteous enthusiasm and the ferocious indignation—found its truest expression in caricature.

Banville described Félix's work during this period with a fond but keen eye: "A heap of astonishing bizarre masterpieces—absurd, crazy, naïve, insolent, charming—that had nothing to do with the art of Raphael and resembled the drawings of a wickedly smart child." Many of his cartoons from 1849 are incomprehensible to anyone not intimately familiar with the extensive cast of Second Republic politicians. But no detailed historical knowledge is required to see him growing in confidence. This may have been the result of a couple of lessons with an accomplished artist specializing in history painting—the only formal instruction Félix ever received. His illustrations grew larger and more sophisticated, their prominent placement proof of his popularity. Banville tells the story of going with the Goncourt brothers to visit Paul Gavarni, the dean of French illustrators, who said to them right away with a look of genuine sadness, "All is lost! See how Nadar has learned to draw!" Although Banville was right to discourage comparisons with Raphael, Félix's graphic skills had noticeably improved. And his name shortened: the *d* had dropped definitively off the end of our hero's pseudonym—he was at last Nadar.

<hr />

NO AMOUNT OF ridicule could slow Louis-Napoléon's rise to power. Elected to the presidency in December 1848 by a huge majority, he claimed for himself the title of Prince-President. Censorship laws had been greatly relaxed after the fall of the monarchy, and this new freedom lasted for another two years, during which time there appeared dozens and dozens of caricatures satirizing the Prince for a Laugh, drawings signed with Nadar's *N*. At the end of 1851, faced with a constitutional term limit, Louis-Napoléon orchestrated a coup d'état that led a year later to his coronation as Napoléon III and the establishment of the Second Empire. He muzzled the press, which meant the shuttering of *La Revue comique* and the abrupt end of Félix's career as a political caricaturist. Tight censorship laws remained in place until after the Franco-Prussian War in 1870.

A few months after the election of the prince-president, Félix jumped ship, abandoning Hetzel for the more pragmatic and successful Philipon. Starting in May 1849, Félix began to contribute regularly to the *Journal pour rire* (Journal for a Laugh), a weekly established by Philipon just weeks before the revolution of February 1848 and now flourishing with a circulation of about fourteen thousand, of which eight thousand were subscribers. (The paper lasted, under one name or another, for more than eighty-five years—a stable venue at last!) Félix's debut was a spectacular effort: a sinuous lineup of sixty delegates to the Constituent Assembly, each one caricatured.

DÉMÉNAGEMENT DE L'ASSEMBLÉE CONSTITUANTE, — dessiné par NADARD, gravé par POTHEY.

Pleased with his new protégé, Philipon slotted Félix into a rotation with three other artists, so that once a month the entire front page of the paper was given over to a Nadar illustration.

Success at the *Journal pour rire* meant that he was busy all the time. Too busy. Other editors were knocking at his door, eager to have the name *Nadar* in their pages; commissions came from all directions. His solution to this happy problem sprang straight from bohemia: he turned his work into a collaborative enterprise. This was the beginning of the "atelier Nadar," an art studio that operated as a factory for turning out newspaper illustrations signed with Nadar's *N*. A half-dozen friends helped out, and family, too: his brother Adrien and a first cousin. Among the rotating crew, one illustrator, Antoine Béguin, was a quasi-permanent fixture. Decades later Félix referred to Béguin as "one of the most fecund of the collaborators who—why not say it?—established the name of Nadar caricatures." He added, with the easy modesty of a man whose fame is secure, that he played his own little part in the enterprise.

The production of images intended for newspaper publication entailed a necessary element of collaboration: for wood engraving, the most common procedure, the artist's drawing had to be transferred onto a wood block, often by a poorly paid third party, then carved by a specialist engraver for the printer. Félix was particularly relaxed about whose hand held the pen when a quick sketch became a finished drawing, and he was not at all fussy about who transferred the work onto the printer's block. There were often two credits at the bottom of an elaborate illustration, one for the artist, one for the engraver.

Félix was always busy, always late, always in demand—and yet always scrambling after money and for more work to bring in more money. In the summer of 1850, he should have been flush: he was already a valued contributor at the *Journal pour rire*, and was also beginning his profitable association with Jean Commerson's satirical weekly, *Tintamarre*. But precisely at that moment he was locked away for a month in the Clichy debtor's prison. A year later he spent a mad three weeks in London during the Great Exhibition of 1851, first aiming to get work with the French-language edition of the *Illustrated London News*, then plotting to launch a rival paper, also in French. The second plan, hatched with his friend Bataille, was a pipe dream. The failure of the first—a perfectly plausible plan, given the excitement generated by the exhibition and the popularity of Nadar's caricatures—was thwarted by the absolute refusal of the editor of the French edition, Constantin Guys, to work with Félix. The mere mention of the name Nadar caused him to exclaim, "Bohemia! Bohemia! One can't count on those people. I won't have it." (This was the same Guys whom Baudelaire later hailed as "the painter of modern life"; he and Félix eventually became close friends.)

When Louis-Napoléon clamped down on the press and expressly banned political caricature, Félix, urged on by Philipon, revisited the idea that had brought him his first success as an illustrator: less than two months after strict censorship was reimposed, he inaugurated a series called *Lanterne magique* (Magic Lantern), an elegant variation on his *Galerie des gens de lettres*.

Each installment consisted of up to eight oblong panels, and on each panel were five or occasionally six caricatures, figures arrayed as though on a slide for use in a magic lantern. Below the panel, a thick block of text provided commentary on the individuals portrayed, a few sentences each, generally humorous. At first only authors and journalists were included, but eventually the series, divided into a dozen installments published over eleven months, embraced painters and musicians as well. By the end, the parade stretched to more than three hundred caricatures, a significant portion of the city's major cultural figures readied for illumination by Nadar's *Lanterne magique*. Implicit in the conceit of the magic lantern is the idea that Félix was offering a privileged glimpse of his milieu: a sneak preview of the slide—with commentary—before its insertion into a device that would project the image for the general public. Also implicit is the parallel between the way a magic lantern enlarges an image on a slide and the publicity generated when a newspaper prints a successful caricature of a public figure. In short, Nadar was operating a machine for magnifying the exposure of celebrities.

The very first panel features Victor Hugo on the road to Mount Parnassus, home of the muses, with friends and family clinging to his coattails. (Hugo had fled Paris a week after the coup d'état, having denounced Louis-Napoléon as a traitor, a principled stand that in Félix's mind transformed the author of *The Hunchback of Notre-Dame* into a hero.)

In the second panel, two of Félix's good friends, Banville and Murger, are joined by a long-legged figure seated on a stack of books, a writing pen, a draughtsman's pencil, and a copy of *Journal pour rire* nearby: it's Félix Tournachon himself, with a mischievous look on his face.

The caption provides the names of his books, identifies him as one of the more active contributors to the *Revue comique*, and mentions helpfully that he's as happy to work with a crayon as a pen. "We regret," the caption concludes, "that we know him too well to say here all the good things we think about him." The drawing is signed, just below the stack of books, not with his usual florid *N* but rather the entire pseudonym—the name *Nadar* was now well on its way to becoming a trademark.

The *Lanterne magique* was another collaborative effort. In order to prepare his remarks on Hugo and his circle, Félix sent his drawings to Auguste Vacquerie, a devoted friend of Hugo's who is pictured right behind him on the finished panel, and asked for information and suggestions for the caption. Vacquerie sent back entertaining prose sketches that Félix appropriated with only minor cuts and modifications—and no attribution. Vacquerie's letter to Félix (whom he affectionately calls "Nadar-chon") is dated just ten days before the caricatures were published on the front page of the *Journal pour rire*, an indication of the rush in which the *Lanterne magique* was thrown together. The exchange with Vacquerie set the pattern for the rest of the series: Félix made use of as many friends as he could, expanding his network and also relying on his old bohemian buddies. Banville wrote a number of the later captions, and Baudelaire was involved as well, feeding Félix opinions about the art critics under consideration. It's not hard to imagine the scene in a noisy, smoky café, a chattering Félix at a crowded table passing around a sheet covered with sketches, asking for advice, improvements, ideas for captions. His pals pick up the pen or the crayon, and little by little a panel takes shape, annotated with useful observations and clever quips.

The Goncourt brothers, who were generally disdainful of Félix in his early days, recorded in their journal an anecdote about his intervention at a party organized early in 1852 by their cousin Count Charles de Villedeuil to mark the launch of his new magazine, *L'Éclair*. Villedeuil had raised funds for the magazine from a moneylender; included in the deal were two hundred bottles of champagne that needed drinking, so Villedeuil decided to share them with his subscribers. According to the invariably snobbish Goncourts, the event, held in the magazine's ground-floor offices, attracted a motley crew of guests: a quintessentially bohemian painter named Pouthier, an unemployed architect, an art dealer, and some girls picked up at a public dance. Also on hand was Félix, who'd been hired to produce a series of caricatures for the magazine. Faced with this drab gathering, he had an idea that was Félix through and through: to make sure the champagne would get drunk, to inject some life into the party, and possibly to needle the aristocratic Villedeuil and his haughty cousins, he opened the shutters on the office windows and began inviting passersby to come in off the street for a glass of fizz.

OF ALL HIS COLLABORATORS, whether they were family, friends, or employees, none was more important than Philipon—not in the sense that the boss involved himself in the creative process (though he did from time to time make suggestions) but rather that he tried his best to steer Félix along a responsible, grown-up path. Philipon was himself a talented caricaturist, as inventive and energetic as Félix. In fact, they had a great deal in common: Philipon was handsome, charming, stubborn, tirelessly energetic, fierce when angered, full of sympathy, much loved by his friends, and famously generous.

But he had one quality that Félix lacked entirely: he was an astute businessman. Being stubborn and kindly, he was relentless in his efforts to convince his protégé that wit and verve should be harnessed to sound commercial practice and sensible work habits. He hoped to instill respect for steady industry (as opposed to frenzied last-minute heroics) and professionalism. His letters to Félix were tough but affectionate, often exasperated, often scolding; the great

majority were aimed at hurrying up a chronically late contributor. (Félix was especially slow in producing captions, further evidence that his difficulty with writing persisted even after his career as an illustrator was firmly established.) Philipon was also careful to point out the dangers of Félix's loud political radicalism, both to the paper and to Félix himself.

Occasionally, Philipon's attempts to impose order on Félix's erratic work habits had some temporary effect. In September 1852, in an entirely unbohemian maneuver, Félix drew up a legal contract defining the exact nature of his collaboration with Antoine Béguin. They entered into a solemn agreement whereby profits from any labor jointly "conceived, prepared and executed" would be divided into three parts, two of which would go to Félix, one to Béguin. Both parties were to devote their day to the partnership "from nine in the morning until five in the evening"; time wasting was to be fined at the rate of one franc per hour. Though this lopsided arrangement endured for many years, with Béguin acting as the foreman of the harum-scarum factory that churned out Nadar drawings, it's safe to say that no fines were ever levied for absenteeism.

Professionalism, meticulous planning, sustained hard work—had Félix been capable of all those things at once, he might possibly have succeeded with the grandiose scheme he hatched at the very end of 1851, when censorship killed off political caricature. He conceived of a series of four outsize lithographs depicting twelve hundred French luminaries—writers, playwrights, artists, musicians—with a separate sheet devoted to each category. According to an early prospectus, the caricatures would be "framed by a tart text," the kind of cheeky biographical commentary that accompanied the *Lanterne magique*. An illustrated who's who of the nation's cultural life, the *Panthéon-Nadar,* as he called it, bore all the hallmarks of Nadar at his best and worst.

The concept was brilliant, the execution a shambles. Félix understood intuitively the emerging celebrity culture, the desire to be publicly known, to be visible and recognized now and in the future. Long familiar with that craving in himself, he could spot it with ease in his contemporaries. To be included in the *Panthéon-Nadar* would be proof of current celebrity, a gratifying confirmation of one's place among the elect. But the judgment of posterity is notoriously fickle, and this uncertainty would introduce an element of tension and drama: could these candidates for posthumous fame be at all confident of admission into *tomorrow's* pantheon? Taking his cue from formal depictions of funeral precessions, Félix decided he would assemble a long snaking line, a cortege doubling back on itself twice: four crowded rows of quietly hopeful contenders on display.

The idea was to present an expectant crowd without giving the impression that the individuals were anxious about their status. (To jockey for position would be beneath the dignity of a true celebrity.)

Between the conception and the reality falls the shadow—in this case the shadow of poorly managed business affairs and the by-now-familiar problem of writer's block. Félix brought to his new project a whirl of energy and his usual uncanny knack for publicity. Over the course of two years, he spent many thousands of francs advertising his *Panthéon* (by June 1853, word of its imminent appearance had even reached the *New-York Daily Times*), but he never managed to complete even a quarter of the work he'd planned and announced. In the end only one sheet was finished (depicting writers and journalists), and it consisted of 250 caricatures, not the three hundred he'd envisioned.

Félix was always ahead of himself. In an announcement published in Villedeuil's *L'Éclair* in the fall of 1852, he offered for sale subscriptions to his four-part *Panthéon* (at thirty francs each)—without giving any indication of when the lithographs would be delivered to the subscriber. The prospectus, signed by the commercial director of *L'Éclair*, indicated that the subscriptions could be purchased at the magazine's offices. Only one problem: it seems Félix neglected to consult Villedeuil, who in the very next issue of *L'Éclair* disavowed any connection with the *Panthéon-Nadar* and implied that Félix had somehow tricked or blackmailed the magazine's director into signing the prospectus. Faced with this "grave" insult, Félix naturally challenged Villedeuil to a duel. Villedeuil, clearly eager to avoid the shedding of blood (especially his own), proposed that the duel take place in Belgium; Félix replied demanding that he be given "satisfaction" where the insult occurred. Villedeuil decided to play it safe and print a retraction. That was not the end of the affair.

In the spring of 1854, Félix announced via another round of costly advertising that the *Panthéon-Nadar* had appeared—"at last." The repeated delays had become a public joke. Worse, the final advertising blitz left him with heavy debts—this despite the intervention of his old boss, the press baron Polydore Millaud, who a year earlier had bought 620 of Félix's original drawings for the

Panthéon for a cool eight thousand francs. Millaud's munificence opened up lines of credit and also allowed Félix to move himself, his mother, and all his animals into a ground-floor apartment with a large garden at 113, rue Saint-Lazare. This was the first time since his childhood that he had lived in a place he could plausibly think of as home.

Thanks to the tremendous costs associated with his *Panthéon*, by midsummer 1854 he owed some five thousand francs (a debt later wiped clean by Jules Mirès, a flamboyant financier who owned two of the newspapers in which the *Panthéon* had been advertised). And yet Félix could take some satisfaction in the praise lavished on his work in the popular press. Displayed in shop windows, the lithograph drew crowds of admirers who were happy to stand on the sidewalk and peer through the glass, to study the sheet and marvel at the ingenuity of the caricatures. It was the talk of the town—but nobody seemed inclined to buy a copy and take it home.

There were good reasons for this reluctance. The *Panthéon-Nadar* is not particularly pretty; no one would think of it as decorative. The size of the sheet (nearly three feet tall and more than a yard wide) made it cumbersome, and the promised biographical text never materialized. Yet on close inspection it's a remarkable achievement: 250 writers caricatured, each one distinctive, almost all amusingly presented—"less handsome than nature made them," as one critic observed, "but more intriguing."

Another critic called it a "delicious museum of grotesques."

One of those grotesques is Félix himself. He sits casually apart from the cortege, as though he were after all indifferent to the idea of a place in the pantheon. He's staring with pop eyes straight out at the viewer—who can't help but recognize his trademark tufts of facial hair and his long, skinny legs clad in stripy hose.

Just in front of him is a signpost bearing the dedication; it's addressed to a gentleman who "on the eight day of the third month of the year 3067" will be running around like a dog trying to buy at any price a copy of the lithograph—now extremely rare—to help him complete his great work on the historical figures of the nineteenth century. In the dedication, Nadar expresses his regret at not knowing this man from the thirty-first century. Looking again at the artist's self-caricature—those bulging eyes—it seems as though Félix is comically astonished to find himself scrutinized by posterity.

Posterity, meanwhile, has noticed that Gustave Flaubert is not among the throng of celebrities (though his mistress, Louise Colet, is on hand). Prosper Mérimée, a prominent author who wrote the novella *Carmen,* on which Bizet's opera is based, is also absent. One could certainly quibble about the ordering of the ranks in the long parade led by Victor Hugo. Looming above Hugo is a classical bust of George Sand perched proudly on a tall pedestal; Balzac, also represented as a bust, is at the base of Sand's pedestal— figuratively speaking at her feet.

Baudelaire is toward the back of the pack, more than two hundred places behind Hugo.

At the very tail end, a tiny figure is being kicked out of the procession—it's Charles de Villedeuil getting his comeuppance.

One more twist to the tale: a few months after the duel that was never fought, the Goncourt brothers wrote to Félix and said that out of family feeling they must ask not to be included in the *Panthéon*. They later changed their minds, and Félix slotted them in toward the rear. And then someone (one of the Goncourts? Villedeuil himself?) complained to the authorities that Nadar had published his caricature without his permission. The minister of the interior duly blocked any further sale of the *Panthéon-Nadar*. The total number of copies sold? One hundred and thirty-six.

AS PHILIPON WATCHED the commercial prospects of the *Panthéon-Nadar* collapse, slowly at first and then all at once, he must have concluded that the talent on display was of greater importance than the business fiasco. In 1856 he demonstrated his faith in his protégé by starting up a new magazine for Félix to edit. The old *Journal pour rire* became *Journal amusant,* and the new publication was given the title *Petit Journal pour rire.* For the cover of the first issue, Félix came up with a clever variation on a famous painting depicting the birth of Henri IV.

In this version, Nadar stands in front of a bed holding aloft an infant in a jester's hat who's brandishing a sign saying *Petit Journal pour rire.* The infant has Philipon's adult face, as does the figure prostrate on the bed behind, who's covered with a sheet bearing the legend *Journal pour rire:* Philipon has given birth to a mini-Philipon, and the gangly Nadar is the proud father.

Scold and cajole as he might, Philipon never managed to engender in Félix any kind of reliable professionalism. By the same token, he never gave up on him and in 1859, a year after the *Petit Journal pour rire* ceased publication, made him editor in chief of the *Journal amusant*. The rich blend of Philipon's feelings (irritation and disappointment battling fondness and amazement) is nowhere more starkly on display than in a long letter dated October 20, 1860—a little more than a year before his death. He begins with what he knew was a futile attempt to trigger a sense of guilt.

My dear Nadar,

It seems to me that you must be racked by horrible pangs of conscience when you think of the splendid emoluments you earn so badly as the editor in chief of the Journal amusant?

And when you think of the Revue trimestrielle *which, for three years, has never appeared on time?*

[. . .]

You will tell me you are very busy, I know, but I know above all that nothing is less true. You don't work, so you're not busy. . . .

Then he repents:

> *Nadar, Nadar, I recognize the error of my ways, I've been touched by grace, and I'm converted.*
> *There is only one God, there cannot be several.*
> *There is only one Nadar, there's only ever been one, there cannot be several.*
> *The mold for God and the one for Nadar are broken.*
> *It's grim, but that's the way it is, one has to get used to it.*
> *Nadar is and will remain the amiable bohemian that we knew as a youth,—a witty man, but without a shred of reason. Enthusiastic about all things, wanting to do it all, to take it all on and—always tiring of it all and letting it all drop. His life has been—is now—and will end unraveled. . . .*
> *I'll finish with one observation:*
> *From the boulevard, we see what's happening at your place, and everyone remarks that we never see you working.*
> *We'll end up believing, if this continues, that you do nothing.*
> *Hide your nakedness.*

The letter is signed, "Your old friend."

Charles Philipon died on January 25, 1862. Félix closed his eulogy by noting that the cause of death was hypertrophic heart disease: "His heart took up *too much room,* said the doctors. They were right."

Félix lost interest in illustration—he let it drop. He found a new, more exciting way to create a compelling likeness: the photograph. But the death of his mentor played its part, too, signaling for Félix the end of an era. Sir Caricature was no more.

VI

ON RUE SAINT-NADAR

Félix's first photographic studio was outdoors at 113, rue Saint-Lazare. Visitors crossed a ground-floor reception room, decorated with a half-dozen lush romantic paintings by his young friend Gustave Doré, before stepping out into a "ravishingly beautiful" courtyard garden. They would sit or stand in the sun in front of a neutral backdrop, and Félix would get to work, the first and most important task being to charm the sitter into forgetting the camera, a bulky box perched on four rickety legs. When he ducked under the black cloth to peer through the lens, the contraption looked like a giant caped spider staring with a single dark eye—an unnerving instrument.

One of his earliest portraits was of Philipon, whose "likable" face Félix described as "open and benevolent, and at the same time full of subtle mockery." Mockery has the edge over benevolence in the photo. (Mentor and protégé must surely have been sparring playfully only an instant earlier.) Philipon's subtlety is immediately—unsubtly—apparent; he radiates undeceived intelligence. Carelessly elegant, tall, and commanding, he brandishes his cigar at chest height. Behind him, the shadow cast on the backdrop by the bright sun is a perfect caricature: a telling exaggeration of his sharp-nosed, frighteningly acute countenance. The shadow quietly undercuts his dignity and at the same time reminds us of his special genius. Could there be a more apt image of the man who founded *La Silhouette* and *La Caricature*, whose drawing of a monarch morphed into a pear made a regime tremble? Philipon would have waited in the garden while Félix, in his makeshift darkroom, soaked the salted paper print in its bath of chemicals, performing the act of modern alchemy that transformed sunlight into an exact reproduction of a vanished instant.

It was probably on an earlier visit, when Félix sketched Philipon for the *Panthéon-Nadar,* that he convinced his mentor to sign his guest book—his *livre d'or*—an outsize autograph album filling up with poems, drawings, watercolors, bars of music, and clever observations left by friends and acquaintances who'd come to be sketched or photographed. Flipping through it on this occasion, Philipon would have smiled to see how apropos his own contribution was: "It's been said of comedy: *castigat ridendo mores* [one corrects morals by laughing]; one can certainly say it of caricature. It's not more true for one than for the other."

I like to imagine the scene when Félix emerged from the darkroom to show Philipon how cleanly the pose was captured. Standing in the garden admiring the portrait on a bright day in the spring or summer of 1854, they would have seen an image (with built-in caricature!) that communicated not just the older man's likeness but also his spirit, the essence of his character. I like to think that this was the moment when they recognized that photography was not just a hobby or a moneymaking scheme or a passing fad that had caught Félix's fancy. They held in their hands proof (if two such quick-witted and forward-thinking men needed further proof) that photography would become a key component of modern life.

The print was also a map to Félix's immediate future, showing where his talent lay and how best to channel his prodigious energy.

IT WAS THANKS to Adrien that Félix first looked through the lens of a camera. In September 1848, a few months after the romantic absurdity of the Polish expedition, Félix helped his younger brother secure a place in François-Édouard Picot's studio at the École des Beaux-Arts; the idea was that Adrien would learn to make his living as a painter. He never did. A dreamy young man, both spoiled and dominated by his mother, he resembled his older brother— but only if you looked closely. Shorter, with a darker complexion, brown eyes, and mousy hair, Adrien never stood out the way Félix did, and no one seemed to expect anything remarkable from him. Notably lacking his older brother's buoyant good humor, he shuffled along, sometimes pleading for help and counting on his brother's network of friends, sometimes petulantly declaring his independence. His life was marred by failures and collapses—physical, mental, and financial— and also by a protracted and damaging quarrel with Félix, a quarrel that began with a gesture of fraternal generosity.

In 1853 Adrien journeyed to England, Scotland, and Ireland hoping to win commissions as a portraitist, but he returned discouraged. Félix had the idea of paying for his brother to acquire another skill: he arranged an apprenticeship with a talented painter-turned-photographer, Gustave Le Gray, who had himself studied painting under Picot. (The deal cost two hundred francs—half-price because Félix and Le Gray were friendly.)

Amazed and delighted by how quickly Adrien mastered the fundamentals of his new trade, Félix helped him set up a photographic studio at 11, boulevard des Capucines. The plan had been for the brothers to collaborate, but once installed in this new establishment, Adrien decided he would prefer to work on his own. The rejection, however ungracious, barely troubled Félix: this was in the early months of 1854, when the *Panthéon-Nadar* was finally about to be printed, and he was even more frantically busy than usual.

But curiosity got the better of him. He asked Camille d'Arnaud, who had been the editor of the most important fine arts magazine of the time, *L'Artiste,* and was now making a start as a photographer, to show him how it was done—not a formal apprenticeship, just a friendly favor. By April, just a few months after first operating a camera, Félix was a shutterbug. He bought equipment and with d'Arnaud's help set up a rudimentary darkroom at the rue Saint-Lazare. He never forgot the many hours d'Arnaud spent patiently teaching him how to prepare the glass negatives. By the summer of 1855, Félix was soliciting trade through advertisements in the press: he'd become a commercial photographer.

As had everyone else. In 1848 there were just thirteen photographers in Paris offering their services to the general public. Over the next two decades, the number grew to more than 350, with 1855 marking the start of the most rapid expansion. Félix was part of a stampede, a cultural and economic phenomenon sometimes known as photomania.

The extraordinary boom was due in part to excitement over the mere fact of photography. Enthusiasm had been building gradually since the mid-1830s, when rumors began to circulate that Louis Daguerre, building on experiments performed with the inventor Nicéphore Niépce, had developed a chemical process that allowed him to fix and preserve the image produced by a camera obscura. In 1839 the secret of Daguerre's process was made public, announced at a joint meeting in Paris of the Academy of Science and the Beaux Arts Academy. A dozen years later an Englishman, Frederick Scott Archer, invented the collodion-on-glass negative. By the time Félix and Adrien got started, exposure times had been drastically reduced (to less than a couple of seconds), and the mass production of photographs was a reality; the cost of having one's photograph taken had fallen accordingly. This coincided with a general mood of prosperity in the French capital, especially from 1852 to 1857, when a great many people (most of them men)—attracted by the modest initial outlay, the short apprenticeship, and the promise of easy profits—decided to set up studios and declare themselves photographers.

These pioneers occupied an ill-defined social position; they floated somewhere between artisan and technician, merchant and shopkeeper— somewhere between working class and bourgeois. A whiff of disrepute, of the mountebank, clung to them: they engaged in mysterious hocus-pocus and sometimes peddled shoddy, blurred images for which they overcharged. Skeptics scorned them; as one sharp-tongued journalist put it, "The invention of Daguerre is the refuge of the artistically incapable." But the more successful and talented practitioners insisted that photography had "higher ambitions; it feels itself called to a nobler role." True believers (and Félix was one of them) preferred to think of the photographer as part artist, part scientist, bravely exploring a new medium with boundless potential.

Félix had a head start. He'd pondered portraiture for at least a half-dozen years, having studied intently many hundreds of faces. He was utterly at ease with a collaborative process (which all but the tiniest photographic enterprise was bound to be). He had tremendous contacts in the press to help get the word out about his new venture. He understood intuitively the celebrity culture incubating in the French capital. As he later boasted, "I had friendly relations—intimate or benevolent—with all the illustrious people of the time." He saw right away that photographs of celebrities would be hugely popular and profitable. More generally, he was a perfect socioeconomic fit: his father, a publisher from a family of publishers, had been securely bourgeois; but Félix himself, due to his father's bankruptcy and early death, and his own long bohemian dalliance, was in a more equivocal position. He felt no need to strive; nor did he worry about slumming. He was neither precious about his own artistic talent nor disdainful of technical tasks. In these respects, the dubious social standing of the photographer troubled him not at all.

But there was the awkward matter of his brother, who had taken to calling himself Nadar *jeune* (Young Nadar)—a liberty to which Félix vehemently objected. Adrien was struggling to keep his fledgling studio solvent; he hoped that by appropriating his brother's pseudonym, he might ride the coattails of the *Panthéon-Nadar*, which had been a huge critical success (and a financial flop). Again Félix did the generous thing: he returned to 11, boulevard des Capucines, and did his best to put the business back on firm footing. His efforts succeeded—but at a cost. He later wrote: "I brought to it all I could: work, money, personal relations, and my pseudonym, which followed me." In mid-January the brothers quarreled again, and Adrien asked Félix to leave *his* studio, which Félix had thought was *theirs*.

Part of the problem was that Félix—out of the blue—was now a married man. The news came as a surprise to his friends—and to himself. Three weeks after the civil ceremony (which took place on August 11, 1854), he wrote to his classmate Asselineau apologizing for not having told him sooner of his marriage plans—especially since he'd named Asselineau as his "first witness." Félix confided that even an hour before the ceremony he had been unsure whether he would go through with it. In fact, he went through with it twice: exactly a month later, on September 11, he was married again in a religious ceremony at a church on the rue d'Aguesseau.

The bride, Ernestine Constance Lefèvre, was half his age: he was thirty-four; she turned eighteen that summer, a month or so before the marriage contract was drawn up. The younger daughter of a family of devout Protestants, originally from Normandy, Ernestine grew up in calm, sheltered bourgeois comfort in a suburb of Paris. Her mother had died of consumption. Her father, Édouard Lefèvre, had been a manufacturer but was now renting out carriages opposite Adrien's studio on the north side of the boulevard des Capucines, which was how Félix got to know the family.

Ernestine was not a great beauty. The first photograph he took of her dates either from shortly before or shortly after they were married. (The jewelry on the ring finger of her left hand suggests after.) Is the wary, combative expression on her face proof that she knows Félix well—too well—and is determined not to be taken in by his banter? The flared nostril and slight squint (her eyes look straight at the camera) could be signs of irritation—or of a teasing skirmish. She could be flirting with him, pretending to be on her guard when in fact she has already willingly surrendered. My guess is that the pose is ironic, compounded of love and comically exaggerated annoyance. Their marriage lasted fifty-five years, longevity that argues for the resilience and resourcefulness of both husband and wife.

What part did Ernestine's substantial dowry play in Félix's decision to marry? The funds were put to immediate use. Many of his debts were discharged, and six thousand francs were invested in camera equipment for Adrien's new studio (an investment that would complicate and aggravate the looming family quarrel). Even if financial calculations nudged Félix in the direction of matrimony, he quickly understood that his wife would bring him more than ready assets. Although tying himself to Ernestine meant relinquishing some of his bohemian freedoms, once wed he embraced family life without hesitation. When their son Paul was born a year and a half after the wedding, on February 8, 1856, Félix was instantly transformed into a doting father. In the characteristically chatty and openly affectionate letters he sent from Brussels six months after the baby's birth (he was exhibiting his work at a photographic exposition, where he won a gold medal), he sends kisses to his wife ("my good little friend") and asks her to kiss their son: "le petit Nadar."

Traces of his love for her, and hers for him, are conspicuous in their long correspondence. But perhaps his most eloquent love letter is a series of photographs taken three and a half decades after the wedding day, photos in which Ernestine, white haired, dark eyed, delicate, and tender, holds a sprig of violets to her lips. A stroke she suffered three years earlier has left her partially paralyzed, yet her pose is graceful, serene. She is, in this intimate moment, a beautiful woman. Roland Barthes called the portrait "one of the loveliest photographs in the world" (and Nadar the world's greatest photographer), and it's easy to see what appealed to him. One doesn't have to know Ernestine's history, or even that she was married to the notorious bohemian Nadar, to see that she has weathered her share of hardship. Félix liked to call her Madame Bonne (Mrs. Good); here he shares with us the fragile but enduring goodness he saw in her face.

Loyal as well as good, Ernestine took Félix's side in all arguments, whether his antagonist was his brother, his mother, or—much later—their son. The brewing dispute with his brother was made more painful for the newlyweds because Adrien showed no intention of repaying the money from her dowry invested in his stu-

dio. The quarrel grew more complicated still when Félix's mother accused Ernestine of turning her husband against his brother, and announced her immediate departure, with all her furniture, from 113, rue Saint-Lazare. However painful for Félix, Thérèse's angry exit surely made married life simpler for Ernestine.

From the moment her husband made the decision to earn his living as a photographer, Ernestine urged him on. In May 1855, five months after Adrien asked him to leave the studio at 11, boulevard de Capucines, Félix published his first photos destined for the commercial market. He was already dreaming up schemes for a professional studio of his own; as usual, those dreams were heroic in scale. The Péreire brothers, Émile and Isaac, bankers who had come to Félix's rescue when the cost of assembling the *Panthéon-Nadar* began to rise alarmingly, were developing a property on the rue de Rivoli with a view to opening a vast, luxurious hotel, the Grand Hôtel du Louvre; Félix had the idea of installing a huge studio on the roof of the building and funding this establishment with a million francs borrowed from the Péreires and Polydore Millaud. One imagines that Ernestine had some reservations about the scope of the project. According to Félix, he went so far as to sign a lease, but a few weeks later the Péreires "modified" the plans for the building, and the deal was off. Common sense prevailed: in February 1856, Félix registered his new company, Société de photographie artistique Nadar et Cie, and raised two hundred thousand francs in capital; Émile and Isaac Péreire, along with Isaac's son Gustave, were the principal backers. The business would remain—modestly, prudently—on the rue Saint-Lazare.

The studio was expanded and remodeled. If it was too wet or too cold to use the garden, Félix could lead his clients up to attic rooms pierced with generous skylights. The elaborate decorations were a canny blend of bohemian and bourgeois that showed off his cultivated taste without veering into the glitzy pomp of the photographic emporiums recently opened on the boulevards. His art collection was by now impressive; in addition to the Dorés hanging in the ground-floor reception room, he owned paintings by Corot, Jongkind, Daumier, and Géricault, as well as several dozen framed drawings. Ancien régime tables and cabinets, mahogany bookcases, Chinese vases, a profusion of antique carved wood statuettes, a ceramic stove from the sixteenth century, a scattering of velvet armchairs—the ambience was plush and intimate, a welcoming lair for connoisseurs of fine art.

Félix recognized, however, that he would have to produce his own art on a sound commercial basis. He was now a family man with a new and urgent need to make money—and over the next six years, he ran a successful business, earned a good living, and paid out a healthy dividend to his shareholders. The rent on the rue Saint-Lazare property was low, never more than three thousand francs per year, and Félix charged high prices for high-quality, large-format prints (8½ inches by 12) sold to a select clientele. In fact, his pricing was on a sliding scale: his closest friends might pay nothing at all; other friends paid thirty francs; acquaintances, fifty francs; and some well-heeled strangers were charged as much as one hundred francs per sitting. He made a further distinction between sitters who wanted their photos taken for their own personal use and enjoyment and celebrities whose photos would be sold to the public or to newspapers. (Illustrations in the press were now commonly credited to both the engraver and the photographer who initially captured the likeness.)

Although the Société de photographie artistique Nadar et Cie advertised its services in newspapers, and the name *Nadar* was written in giant letters on the wall near the entryway to 113, rue Saint-Lazare, Félix was not particularly interested in luring customers off the street. He had his eyes on the cultural elite, the cast of characters he would have included in the *Panthéon-Nadar* had he completed all four sheets, had the musicians, painters, sculptors, and actors joined the cortege of writers and journalists. In a sense, he was carrying on with that aborted project in a new medium, amassing portrait by portrait a vast gallery of notable Parisians. In 1859 he exhibited sixty of those portraits at a show organized by the Société française de photographie; the verdict of one critic, Philippe Burty, writing in the newly founded *Gazette des beaux-arts,* shows that his contemporaries well understood the scope of his ambition:

> The whole constellation, literary, artistic, dramatic, political—intelligent, in a word—of our era, has filed through his studio; the sun is merely his assistant, Mr. Nadar is the artist who gives him work. The series of portraits he's exhibiting is the Pantheon, serious this time, of our generation.

Friends he made in his bohemian days accounted for a sizable portion of his new clientele, and they ensured that word of mouth was his best publicity. Profoundly impressed by the images he produced, they paid him the handsome compliment of renaming the street in his honor: they spread the word that if you were an artist of any stature, the place to have your photograph taken was "the rue Saint-Nadar."

Financiers (especially those who had lent him money or might do so in the future) were also invited to join Nadar's photographic

Pantheon, as were some generals, foreign ambassadors, and well-connected tourists. Very few aristocrats sat for Nadar, none of the courtiers of Napoléon III, and none of the members of the imperial family: Félix's republican loyalties, though selectively engaged, had not withered entirely.

He still opened his doors at all hours to pals he'd met in his youth in cafés and garrets—the habit of generosity never left him—and he still wandered on foot through Paris with the same restless curiosity, but married life and a thriving studio gradually reshaped his bohemian behavior and attitudes. Is it ironic that his most successful years as an artist were also his most profitable as a businessman? If so, the irony is compounded by his insistence, during this prosperous period, that photography was an art, and by his snobbish disdain for those who exploited it as a purely commercial venture. Money often distorted Félix's perspective but rarely in predictable ways.

And never when he was looking through the lens of a camera. For all the noise Félix made over his long lifetime, for all the chatter and the tireless agitation of his several tumultuous careers and many transient enthusiasms, it is the quiet pause, the stillness and silence as he released the camera's shutter, opened and closed in a heartbeat, that makes an irresistible claim on our attention. Proof of his genius, the portraits are his own ticket to the pantheon of great artists.

Part of the excitement of looking at the early photographs is the chance to see an artist who has thoroughly mastered a technique yet still seems to be feeling his way, learning something new with each exposure.

His schoolmate Charles Asselineau, a bibliophile steeped in literature, an early and ardent champion of Baudelaire's poetry, strikes a meditative pose, as though he were completely alone. He's turned his head to the side, and only half his broad face is illuminated; he seems unaware of the camera. Photographing an old and dear friend, Félix has managed to vanish from the scene; the interaction that's so essential in other portraits plays no part here. With his thick, curly beard and a stocky body that claims nearly all the space in the photo, Asselineau is unmistakably masculine, yet the mood of the portrait is tender, mildly melancholy, and faintly feminine, like the floral pattern on the fabric of the sofa where he's lounging (a piece of furniture that reappears in other portraits). The hand on his lap is slightly blurred, soft and unsettled, maybe a little sad. Asselineau was known for his generosity and his gentle manners, and this is what Nadar shows us.

Another early portrait presents a middle-aged Théophile Gautier, portly, messy, unbuttoned in every respect, dressed in an exotic pale robe over a pale shirt open at the neck, sporting a loosely knotted, flamboyantly striped foulard. With one hand buried to the wrist down the front of his trousers—an insolent gesture just shy of obscene—this could only be a bohemian, an artist proud to be wild and unconventional, a devotee of art for art's sake. The imposing, fleshy face, thickly bearded, is turned slightly to the left; under a prominent brow and a broad, brightly lit forehead, the eyes, baggy and shaded, look off into the distance. It's not that he's unaware of the camera—he's snubbing it. Félix had a nickname for his friend Théophile: "Le Théos," as in the Greek for "god." There's a fittingly casual arrogance to his pose: he's not a man to doubt his power. Already celebrated as a poet, novelist, critic, playwright, and travel writer, he's not quite at the peak of his fame—that will come a decade later, in the 1860s—but he has no reason to question himself or doubt that he'll enjoy the approving judgment of posterity.

The poet Marceline Desbordes-Valmore, a tiny elderly woman, sits on the same sofa where Asselineau posed. She is as famous as Gautier and well respected by critics, yet there's not a trace of arrogance or self-satisfaction in her expression. She sits up, her head

canted to the side, her eyes brimming with emotion, her lips slightly parted—surely she's about to speak. The question is not what she'll say but why she so urgently feels the need to communicate. Her poems are flavored by melancholy, and so is Nadar's portrait, the sadness thrown into relief by the jaunty finery of her dress, the elaborate white lace sleeves and the fingerless black lace gloves.

There are dozens and dozens of other portraits equally astonishing in their immediacy, not only of famous figures (a hungry Baudelaire, a cocky Dumas, a monolithic Daumier) but also of ordinary people: Ernestine's schoolteacher, a delicate, freckled young woman decked out in black lace; a black woman called Maria, draped in a velvet wrap in one photo, her sumptuous breasts exposed in another; an anonymous young woman, probably a friend's mistress, in that same velvet wrap, with her luxuriantly frizzy hair let loose. All these images, austerely focused on human essence, are the fruit of the miraculous years on the rue Saint-Nadar.

What does it do for us to look at these photos of men and women who died so long ago? Barthes confessed that his fascination with photography was "tinged with necrophilia . . . a fascination with what has died but is represented as wanting to be alive." Perhaps we all feel something similar: we say that Nadar's subjects are "brought to life," but that's just figurative shorthand for a more complicated sense that looking at their faces, their clothes, perhaps their hands, we learn something about who they were and what it was like to sit beside them. We hope we're making some kind of connection with a vanished era. It's an illusion, of course, just like the idea that a photograph is "real" in a way an oil portrait is not. We can't really know someone by peering at a photograph taken 150 years ago (or at a selfie taken fifteen minutes ago). Yet the magic of Nadar's portraits—their sincerity, their freshness, their unwavering faith in the possibility of capturing a piercingly accurate psychological likeness—tempts us to forget our skepticism, to look past the sepia tint, the old-style hats and coats, and our doubts about the veracity of photographic images. We're tempted, when we first see them, to trust the spark of recognition, that instant when we come face to face with a fellow being who's alive and knowable.

The person Félix photographed most frequently was himself—

out of curiosity more than vanity. He experimented on himself, attempting to push portraiture as far as it would go in its fundamental mission of revealing identity. In other words, he tried, fitfully, to set aside his habitual showmanship and show who he was. He worked at a disadvantage: there was no one to charm him out of his self-consciousness—he couldn't be expected to banter with himself—and he was notoriously bad at holding still: the real Félix was in constant motion, frenetic energy a defining element of his personality. Was he the same man when frozen in place? If Nadar asked a friend to sit for him, he would manipulate the pose and the lighting, chatting away all the while, then step back and examine the result. When he sat for himself, with an assistant releasing the shutter, he could gauge the effectiveness of the pose only after the print was developed. And ironically his eyesight was poor: behind the camera he wore his spectacles, but in front of it he removed them. (You sometimes see them in portraits dangling from a ribbon around his neck.) Sitting for a self-portrait, he was in a sense doubly blind to the goings-on.

Often what we get is only a glimpse of a certain aspect of his personality. The very earliest self-portraits mostly show eagerness. Still unsure of his technique, he wanted the image to prove at least recognizable: apprehension mixes with impatience and desire to produce nothing more than a fuzzy, pleading look on the face of a bohemian no longer in his first youth. As his confidence grew, his ambition asserted itself, and he achieved specific calculated effects. In a striking seated portrait, he looks directly at the camera and attempts—perhaps too transparently—to seduce the viewer with his charm.

He tilts his head forward and slightly to the side, rests his cheek on his hand, and fixes you with one hopeful eye. (The other is deep in shadow.) He appeals silently for an intimate exchange. Although his hair is uncombed, he's more neatly dressed than usual, his black cravat crisp against the white of his shirt. If he's aiming for sincerity, he has missed the mark; the result is more coy than genuine.

In another early self-portrait he stands tall, his body at an angle to the camera, arms crossed and hands buried in the sleeves of his jacket, head swiveled so that he looks back over his shoulder.

It's a theatrical pose with heroic overtones: behold Nadar as romantic artist, isolated, exposed, self-contained, self-protective, ready to move forward, but conscious of what's behind him— which in this case might be the painterly tradition of portraiture.

A hint of vulnerability, of anxiety in the eyes and around the mouth, adds considerably to the interest of the photograph. Was Félix truly anxious? Or is this a deliberate imitation of troubled genius?

The best photos of Félix aren't formal self-portraits. A photomontage of our hero dancing the can-can on the tip-top of a steeple (or is it the point of an ink pen?), an absurd image that caricatures Félix's long legs and somehow catches his anarchic spirit: he's wild-eyed, wild-haired, astonished, and worried about his precarious position. I don't know who did the cut-and-paste job, splicing comically elongated limbs onto a Nadar self-portrait, or who inscribed it to whom (the inscription reads, "To the great man/ the instant daguerreotype/ with gratitude"), but my guess is that it was a present to Félix from a waggish friend.

The other revelatory portrait is an experiment in making moving pictures: a dozen photos of Félix from the chest up, taken from twelve successive angles—flip through them and you have a revolving portrait.

In the sixth photo, when he's just about to face the camera straight on, he grins; in the next photo the sly smile is gone, replaced by a level stare.

The effect is like a playful wink or a wave, a subtle subversive signal to posterity. Hardly anybody smiled for the camera in the mid-nineteenth century; to do so was to risk appearing foolish or simple-minded. Today's ubiquitous smirk was unthinkable. Yet Félix, unwilling or unable to smother his high spirits, flashed his grin—and so left proof that the friends who celebrated his boisterous good humor understood him best. It's the confirmation of Baudelaire's remark: "Nadar, the most astonishing expression of vitality."

VII

NADAR VS. NADAR JEUNE

W HEN FÉLIX WAS NEWLY MARRIED, THE FOND
father of a baby boy, and was running a profitable
studio with an enviable reputation, he seemed incapable of producing an uninteresting photograph. It was a charmed
period of domestic contentment and professional success crowned
by artistic triumph—but it was marred by an epic feud with Adrien
that began in 1854 and escalated two years later into a legal battle
not definitively resolved until mid-1859. Is it accidental that Félix's
remarkable spurt of creativity coincided with a fierce family fight, a
dispute that involved both his sense of self and his ambitions for the
future? There are no telltale traces of discord in his best work from
those years, but it seems clear that the struggle spurred him on and
shaped his art in a fundamental way.

The bitterness of long-simmering sibling rivalry makes it hard
to grasp the exact contours of the quarrel. In its simplest form, it
was about Félix's pseudonym, which Adrien had co-opted as soon
as he was set up in his studio at 11, boulevard des Capucines, advertising himself as both Adrien Tournachon and Nadar *jeune*.
Félix complained, worried that the appearance of this new, ersatz
Nadar would complicate his efforts to market the *Panthéon-Nadar*.
Six months later, when Adrien's fledgling enterprise appeared to be
faltering, Félix agreed to help out at the studio, at which point he
allowed (and possibly encouraged) his brother to stamp his prints
Nadar jne, calculating that the use of the pseudonym would improve
Adrien's prospects—and therefore his own. He and Ernestine had

invested generously in the venture and wanted Adrien to succeed, if only to safeguard their investment. But it proved impossible for the two brothers to work together. One can easily imagine the scene: the irrepressible Félix bossing his sibling around as though he were one of the assistants, offering his advice at every turn; the moody, envious Adrien moping, seething with resentment.

They rubbed along uncomfortably from September 1854 until January 1855, four months during which dozens of extraordinary photographs were produced in the studio, some of them procuring for Adrien a gold medal at the 1855 Exposition Universelle (after Félix pulled strings to get the work into the show). Whose work was it? Attributing specific photos to one brother or the other is mostly a matter of guesswork; often the attribution turns on a printing technique used by Adrien but not by Félix. But just because Adrien produced the print and signed it *Nadar jne* doesn't mean that Félix wasn't involved in creating the image.

For example, the famous *Pierrot* series featuring the mime Charles Deburau *fils* dressed as Pierrot striking a variety of dramatic poses: Pierrot photographer, Pierrot running, Pierrot in pain, Pierrot laughing. Adrien may have released the shutter, done the darkroom work, and stamped the print with his (assumed) name, but Félix would have had his say about which poses the mime struck; he would have had opinions, forcefully expressed, about the

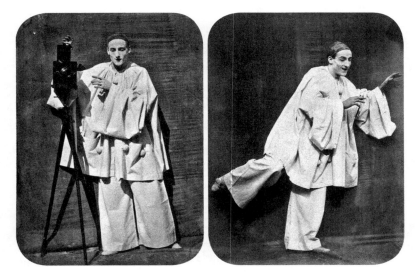

lighting and composition of each shot. Félix was in fact responsible for the presence of Deburau in the studio—it was he who issued the invitation, thinking that photographs of the mime would make a novel study.

The same goes for the artists and literary figures whose portraits have in recent decades been attributed to Adrien. Does it make any sense to give the younger brother sole credit for the haunting photo of a despairing Nerval? It's true that Adrien took the editor of *L'Artiste* to court for printing an illustration of Nerval based on the portrait without giving him credit or paying him, which seems to some scholars conclusive evidence that the photo was Adrien's. But Nerval was a friend and colleague of Félix, not Adrien; the composition of the portrait and its psychological depth are classic Nadar; and Félix later wrote about the image as though he alone were its author. (Somewhat unfairly, he called it "a saddening photograph that renders neither the simplicity nor the subtlety nor the charm of the sitter.") Is it any surprise that contradictory claims surround the fruit of a fractious collaboration, or that confusion and uncertainty reign?

One of the portraits now attributed to Adrien is of Charles Augeron, the schoolmaster who housed and cared for a teenage Félix after his father, mother, and brother left Paris for Lyon. It's difficult to imagine that Augeron would have preferred to sit for Adrien rather than Félix (who referred to the schoolmaster as "the man who had so charitably replaced my dead father")—but if indeed the younger brother was solely in charge of the session, that might explain why the portrait is stiff and the unsmiling subject apparently ill at ease. There's no sign here of the benign surrogate parent whose kindness and compassion kept a troubled boy off the streets.

There are two versions of the superb early portrait of Gustave Doré, identical except that one was printed by Félix, one by Adrien. Again, the bond of friendship was with Félix, who had met Doré six years earlier, when the artist was a fifteen-year-old prodigy working as an illustrator for Philipon. One glance tells you that this is a Nadar portrait: watchful, anxiously brooding, the twenty-one-year-old Doré offers the camera a sullen challenge. Wrapped in a heavy, funereal coat, half his face shaded, he seems to emerge from mystery; the shadow he casts on the backdrop emphasizes his wispy, unkempt beard and tangled eyebrows. (The hair on his head is also untidy.) By concentrating the action in a small portion of the photo, Nadar gives the impression of a young man on the verge: if Doré's confidence builds, the photo suggests, he'll break out with considerable force, filling with youthful energy the empty space around him. (Always staggeringly prolific, within a decade Doré would be the most celebrated illustrator in France.)

The fact that Adrien printed a copy of the Doré portrait and stamped it *Nadar jne* suggests to me not that he had a hand in making the image but that he was unscrupulous in claiming credit for work that wasn't his.

And then there's the striking portrait of Adrien himself in a smock and straw hat, dressed as though he were an artist sketching en plein air, bathed in warm sunshine, his chin in his hand, a cigarette dangling from his lips. A dreamy image of *dolce far niente*, of a sensitive soul in calm repose, utterly detached from the busy grind of bourgeois life. It's a photograph about reverie, and it invites speculation. Is this lazy Adrien's fantasy of the artist's life? Or is it Félix's fantasy of his brother finally finding inspiration and achieving a serene success—without actually having to do any work? Impossible to say with any certainty.

Disagreement today about attribution seems like a continuation of the sibling spat, which flared up again in the third week of 1855,

when Adrien declared that he wanted Félix out of the studio at 11, boulevard des Capucines. Stung, the older brother retreated to the rue Saint-Lazare, demanding his name back—as well as the six thousand francs he and Ernestine had invested. Adrien refused on both counts. In February, Félix proposed arbitration, but no settlement could be reached. Adrien, meanwhile, was planning to form a new studio with new backers, both of them musicians: the baritone Jules Lefort and the celebrated organist Louis Lefébure-Wély. His two partners invested thirty thousand francs each; Adrien contributed the equipment, furnishings, and clientele from his existing studio, along with his contested name. The new business, Société Tournachon Nadar et Cie (note the absence of *jeune*), was incorporated in October 1855 and opened its doors several months later in grander premises on the teeming boulevard des Italiens. A worldly character, Lefébure-Wély directed a stream of fashionable clients to the studio, including Empress Eugénie.

Perhaps it was the public linking of his pseudonym with the imperial court that drove Félix to seek legal redress, or perhaps it was the news that Adrien had reordered several thousand engraved business cards bearing the name *Nadar jne*—either way, Félix was driven to drastic action: he dispatched bailiffs to seize the cards at the printer and launched a lawsuit claiming trademark protection for his pseudonym, and he filed a statement with the court that's more like a howl of protest than a legal document. As he explained to the tribunal, the fundamental issue at stake was his identity: "I find myself first having to prove that I am me." His pseudonym, adopted nearly twenty years earlier, was "more my name than my name"—he was not Tournachon but Nadar, and now his brother was trying to steal Nadar, his very essence.

The tribunal ignored his howl. The judgment handed down on April 23, 1856, allowed Adrien to continue to use the name *Nadar* on the following grounds: the younger sibling had earned a reputation as a photographer using the name *Nadar;* he had won a prize at the Exposition Universelle using the name *Nadar;* and as a result Félix could not justly claim exclusive use of the name, especially as he had in correspondence referred to his brother as "Nadar *jeune.*"

The judges weren't wrong about these specific points. They might also have pointed out that Félix had originally encouraged his brother to become a photographer and, once he'd invested in the studio on the boulevard des Capucines, allowed Adrien to adopt the moniker *Nadar jeune.* He'd been hoping to profit from Adrien's change of profession (if only in the meager sense that a self-sufficient Adrien would no longer be a drain on his finances). At the very least Félix was inconsistent in his attitude toward his brother's use of the pseudonym. And he was clearly conflicted about his brother's success. Was it because Adrien showed glimmers of talent as a photographer that Félix decided to set up a darkroom and exhibit his own skill? If Adrien's success with photography was a goad to Félix, Félix's success must have been intolerable to his younger brother.

Which may help explain some of the devious and dishonest behavior Adrien engaged in during these years. Having asked his older brother to leave the boulevard des Capucines, Adrien showcased portraits made by Félix in the windows of his own studio; he let it be known to credulous clients that he was in fact the true Nadar—the man of letters, the caricaturist, the creator of the *Panthéon-Nadar*. Later, when he moved to the new studio on the boulevard des Italiens, he hung out a banner advertising the premises as the home of *Nadar jne*—but made the *jne* so tiny that a casual glance would miss it entirely; and he modified the *Nadar jne* signature that he stamped on his prints so that it looked very much like Félix's *Nadar*. This kind of petty subterfuge infuriated Félix and made him all the more intent on securing a favorable legal judgment.

He launched a formal appeal and organized a campaign in the press promoting the studio on the rue Saint-Lazare as the true home of Nadar. A year and a half later, on December 12, 1857, the court found in Félix's favor and ordered Adrien to stop using his older brother's pseudonym. Adrien in turn appealed—without success. The final judgment, handed down on June 6, 1859, reaffirmed Félix's exclusive right to the pseudonym.

Félix had won. While Adrien's career petered out, his older brother, already the most famous photographer in Paris, established himself as a great portraitist—and that may have been the point all along.

The feud with Adrien revealed a darker side of Félix's character, a taste for conflict and confrontation that would surface again and again in his later years: he carried grudges and reveled in polemic excess. Sometimes it seemed as if he picked fights precisely so that he could unleash a prose tirade. Consider the furious assault on Champfleury early in 1859, more than a decade after their skirmish over Champfleury's nasty review of Félix's pantomime, *Pierrot Ministre*. This time Félix produced a prose sketch of his antagonist, a brief biography (one of a series called "Nadar's Contemporaries" published in Philipon's *Journal amusant*) that had some slight legitimacy as criticism but quickly gave way to ad hominem attack. At issue was Balzac's literary legacy. Félix described Champfleury running over to Balzac's house while the great man's corpse was barely cold and snatching up whatever odds and ends he could find: bits of ironwork, broken pots, cigar butts—"he even ran across an old pair of the dead man's shoes, and shoved his feet in them right away." Any reader who kept up with literary gossip would have instantly recognized an allusion to Champfleury's brief affair with Balzac's widow, Ewelina Hańska, who was twenty years older than Champfleury. And that jab was witty in comparison with what followed: Félix accused his victim of simply not knowing how to write French and dismissed him as vain, self-satisfied, and ridiculous.

Adrien made a successful portrait of Champfleury squinting into the distance with heroic intensity and drawing on his cigar, a fearsome furrow on his brow.

Several years later, probably after Félix's blast in *Journal amusant*, Champfleury came to the rue Saint-Lazare and sat for his Nadar portrait. The result is unusual and somewhat comical: the sitter looks at the camera with apparent distrust, his chin drawn in and his mouth twisted as though he's swallowed something nasty—perhaps his pride. He's notably absent from Félix's *livre d'or*. Did Félix not offer him the chance to sign, or did Champfleury refuse?

What's clear is that to galvanize his energies, Félix needed an adversary, whether it was Champfleury, Louis-Napoléon, or his own hapless brother. Battling with Adrien stirred him up and egged him on; it also concentrated his mind and caused him to set down on paper his ideas about the art form he was fighting over. In his appeal against the tribunal's initial judgment, he wrote with reckless vehemence about his new profession:

> Photography is a marvelous discovery, a science that engages the most elevated intellects, an art that sharpens the wits of the wisest souls—the practical application of which lies within the capacity of the shallowest imbecile. This prodigious art which out of nothing makes something, this miraculous invention after which anything seems possible, this Photography which with applied Electricity and Chloroform makes our nineteenth century the greatest of all centuries—this supernatural Photography is practiced on a daily basis. . . . The theory of photography can be learned in one hour; the basic practice in one day.

This much can be learned . . . which means that anyone, without exception, can safely aspire to call himself a photographer by tomorrow at the latest.

I am going to tell you what cannot be learned: it's a feel for light—it's the artistic appreciation of the effects produced by various qualities of lighting alone or combined—it's the application of this or that effect according to the nature of the physiognomy that as an artist you aim to reproduce.

What is even less likely to be learned is the moral intelligence of your subject—the rapid tact that puts you in communion with your model . . . and allows you to give . . . a more familiar and favorable resemblance, the intimate resemblance—that's the psychological aspect of photography, the word seems to me not too ambitious.

He goes on to say that there's another quality that can't be learned: "zeal [and] tireless work in the fierce and persistent pursuit of what's *better*"—a hunger for excellence that he associates with essential probity and honesty—honesty of the sort that "has its eye not on today but on all the tomorrows."

That's as close as he ever came to issuing an artistic manifesto—and it's contained in a legal document submitted to the court in a lawsuit against his brother.

VIII

ON THE BOULEVARD

"But who or what can stop me once I've embarked
on one of my enthusiasms?"

—NADAR

GUSTAVE LE GRAY, THE PAINTER-TURNED-PHOTOG-rapher who taught Adrien and scores of others how to take pictures, made a fateful decision in 1855, just as Félix was establishing himself on the rue Saint-Lazare. Le Gray decided to relocate his photographic studio to a brand-new two-story building on the boulevard des Capucines, near the corner of the rue Neuve Saint-Augustin (now the rue Daunou). He was by this time one of the leading photographers in Paris, with a fashionable clientele for his portraits; discerning buyers paid high prices for his forest landscapes, his streetscapes, and his lush seascapes. He had benefited early on from state sponsorship, receiving commissions to photograph national monuments, including the châteaux of the Loire and the medieval fortifications of Carcassonne. Now, backed by funds from a noble family from Normandy (the comte de Briges invested one hundred thousand francs), Le Gray resolved to exploit his success by setting up shop in the commercial heart of the city. Expensive work was done to the new building, especially to the sumptuously appointed interior. The foyer was lined in Spanish leather. Leading up to the glassed-in studio, the double staircase was draped in fringed crimson velvet. The salon, ostentatiously furnished with antiques, sealed his claim to sophisticated luxury.

Le Gray was neither the first nor the last to fall into this trap. A roll call of pioneer photographers, mesmerized by the prospect of the millions to be made in their new trade, spent far too liberally on constructing and decorating their studios; when the expected millions failed to materialize, they were slowly crushed by debt—or quickly crushed. Many decades later Félix wrote about this inexorable fate with evident sympathy:

> From these preliminary obstacles, even from the formidable installation costs—which will follow and dog you to the end, implacable like all original sins—it would perhaps have been possible to pull free, but only on the condition of having to a high degree that *je ne sais quoi*, that gift, both pedestrian and divine, called business sense. And it's precisely that sense that was lacking in the good Le Gray.

Competition among professional photographers grew fierce in the second half of the decade, with new studios opening daily in the city. With no prospect of a return on their investment, Le Gray's aristocratic backers began exhibiting signs of impatience. To make matters worse, a craze for *cartes de visite*—photographs as calling cards, cheaply produced and sold cheaply by the thousands—cut into the high end of the market: why have your portrait taken in large format for as much as a hundred francs when you could have a dozen *cartes* made up for as little as twenty francs? Popular demand was in this case irresistible. Félix wrote,

> It was a rout. One had to submit, that is to say follow the trend, or quit. It was above all Le Gray's preoccupation with art that had pushed him toward photography; he couldn't resign himself to turning his studio into a factory: he gave up.

In 1860, just five years after his move to the boulevard, Le Gray fled the country. The de Briges family had accused him of allowing himself a too-generous portion of the studio income; creditors were harassing him. Abandoning his wife and children, he embarked with Dumas *père* on an expedition to the Orient. After a detour to Sicily (where he photographed Garibaldi in the midst of the battle for Palermo) and adventures in Malta and Syria, he washed up in Egypt. Opening a modest photographic studio in Cairo, he taught drawing and secured a pasha's patronage. Although he lived until 1884, he never saw Paris again.

Félix told this story in 1890. In his telling, it's a cautionary tale—but the thing about cautionary tales is that they're of little use in hindsight. Back in 1860, when he decided that his fame and talent merited a plush setting and a generous cash flow, he had paid no attention to the dramatic unraveling of Le Gray's career. On the contrary: he agreed to rent 35, boulevard des Capucines, the exact building where Le Gray had established the swank photographic emporium that bankrupted him and drove him into exile.

———————

WHY WOULD FÉLIX want to leave the rue Saint-Lazare? There was a legitimate practical consideration: his thriving business could keep up with the competition only if it grew, and to grow it needed room. He saw this as a pivotal moment in his life, with good cause. His aged mother was sick, and his anxiety at the thought of her death made him eager to trumpet his professional success; he had vanquished his brother and felt that the victory called for a bold gesture; and the lawsuit and his own shrill insistence on the value of the name Nadar gave him an inflated conception of its commercial magic. Familiar quirks of his character also helped push him out the door: his congenital restlessness, undiminished at age forty; his compulsion to think big, then bigger; and his need to face and surmount a challenge (a variation on his need to face and defeat an adversary).

Friends and family urged him to stay put or to expand sensibly. He wasn't listening. When Thérèse Tournachon lay dying of uterine cancer in February 1860, her deathbed wish was that her sons be reconciled. Even gravely ill, she could tell that Adrien was in trouble, and she wanted to be sure that his older brother would look after him. Less than a week before she died, Adrien went bankrupt; the studio on the boulevard des Italiens was shuttered. A dutiful son, Félix paid off part of Adrien's outstanding debt and bought up his material and equipment.

As Félix's plans took shape, Adrien warned from bitter experience against the hazard of high fixed costs. In a letter sent four days after their mother's death, he wrote, "You're taking on a business that is too large for you alone." He added, "I know very well that you won't admit the possibility of failure, but still, would you be the first? . . . Either you will die of overwork, or the leakage that you don't see will scuttle your establishment." The phrase "fixed costs" tolls like a funeral bell.

Predictably deaf to this hard-won wisdom, Félix signed in April a long-term lease on 35, boulevard des Capucines, committing him to paying thirty thousand francs for the first three years and twelve thousand per year thereafter—in other words, his fixed costs were far higher than they'd been on the rue Saint-Lazare. But that was only the beginning, because the studio as he conceived it didn't yet exist. The plan was to build a two-story iron and glass structure on top of the existing building, a grandiose scheme that cost, when completed—six months behind schedule—a staggering 230,000 francs.

He and his family installed themselves in an apartment at the back of the building, overlooking the courtyard, while work on the studio progressed. Félix supervised intermittently, offering the foreman detailed guidance. Once finished, the establishment was extravagant on a scale beyond anything attempted by Gustave Le Gray or any other photographer. In the lobby on the ground floor, open to the boulevard, Nadar's celebrity portraits were proudly displayed; on the third floor were two lavish salons; a corridor decorated with *portraits-charge* by Nadar led to the stairway up to the huge top-floor workspace, just as opulent as the salons and more spectacular. Water flowed in a sheet down the outside of a large glass pane in the ceiling; it was piped into the studio, where it cascaded onto a boulder, cooling the room on hot summer days. In the winter the indoor waterfall was turned off, and the space was heated by the same magnificent sixteenth-century faience stove he'd had at the rue Saint-Lazare. His art collection had expanded to include a fine Gobelins tapestry, many more objets d'art—ancient Chinese porcelain, old jewelry, antique statuettes in carved wood—and countless curiosities housed in glass cases. A pair of baroque Solomonic columns, ornate twists with a vine filigree, completed the crowded, eclectic look. The sharp-tongued

Philipon, writing in *Le Journal amusant,* made merciless fun of Félix's profligacy, especially a set of chairs purchased for six hundred francs apiece—but the mockery was intended to excite his readers' curiosity, to lure them to the studio.

Philipon was keeping a wary eye on the money so freely spent—as well as trying to corral customers—because he was one of the investors. Among the others were sympathetic bankers like the Péreire brothers and old pals who had exchanged their bohemian threads for bourgeois finery: Auguste Lefranc, the playwright-turned-banker, and Hérald de Pages, formerly a hack, now suddenly a landowner. Félix established the Société générale de photographie and sold fifty thousand francs' worth of shares.

Eugène Philipon, Charles's son, took a seat on the corporation's supervisory council. A manager was hired, and a small army of assistants—Félix at one point had as many as fifty people working for him. He set his own salary at one thousand francs a month.

Imagine for a moment that he could shrug off the weight of his accumulated debts—what a thrill to cross the crowded boulevard and gaze at his achievement! As if through force of will he'd erected a handsome modern structure, its well-proportioned pediment topped by three female busts (the graces) sculpted by his friend Émile Blavier. On the facade, his giant signature, faithfully reproduced in glass tubing, was an advertisement, a beacon, and also a token of ownership: *I built this, it's mine.*

The sign was made for Félix by Antoine Lumière, which gives it a modern pedigree in addition to its modern look. Himself a photographer as well as a sign painter, Lumière was the father and business associate of Auguste and Louis, the famous Lumière brothers, who played a key role in the development of cinema. The swooping *Nadar* fashioned by Lumière *père* was red like the interior of the studio—not so subtle by day and positively bling when lit up by gas at night. The sign said the same thing as the ultra-extravagant interior: everything about the studio, when it opened in September 1861, proclaimed Nadar the premier photographer in Paris.

The new establishment was designed to attract a particular clientele: the urban middle class that was still rapidly expanding ten prosperous years into the Second Empire. Although Félix was seeking to profit from the political and economic stability that allowed his customers to thrive, he remained steadfastly hostile to the regime. His chief competitor, André Adolphe-Eugène Disdéri (who patented the procedure for manufacturing photographic *cartes de visite*—and made a fortune from them) was the quasi-official photographer of government ministers and the preferred portraitist of the imperial family. Félix was among the many who told the apocryphal story of Napoléon III marching out of Paris at the head of his army, celebrating with pomp and ceremony the commencement of his Italy campaign, and stopping at Disdéri's studio to have his portrait made in *carte de visite* format while thousands of soldiers waited patiently on the boulevard. As Félix put it, "With that, enthusiasm for Disdéri became a delirium. The entire universe knew his name and the path to his door."

Although he admired Disdéri's commercial instinct and "practical intelligence," Félix was witheringly snobbish about his competitor's lack of artistic talent. Disdéri, he suggested, would have done just as well in some other industry, marketing whatever "product" the factory churned out. He even permitted himself a disparaging remark about Disdéri's unprepossessing looks ("repulsive" is the adjective he chose)—all this to highlight the edgy elegance of Nadar's own studio, his vaunted artistic genius, and his status as the preferred photographer of opposition celebrities. He cultivated an antiestablishment chic meant to entice not only the cultural elite but also anyone who hoped to mix with artists, radicals, and the band of bohemians and ex-bohemians made famous by Murger's *La Vie de Bohème*. The idea was that the new clientele would pay high prices for the glamour of the Nadar brand.

There was precedent for this. Le Gray wasn't the only photographer who had set up shop in 35, boulevard des Capucines; the Bisson brothers, famous for their Alpine photography, had a salesroom there in the late 1850s, a "boutique" where customers would pick up finished prints. The shop was "all the rage," according to Félix:

> It wasn't only the extraordinary luxury and good taste of the furnishings or the novelty and perfection of the products on sale that halted the passerby; there was also lively interest in contemplating . . . the illustrious visitors who succeeded each other on the velvet cushions of a great circular divan, passing around the day's photographs.

Gautier, Baudelaire, and Delacroix, among others, made the Bissons' establishment their rendezvous. Twice Félix saw there the most powerful banker in France, Baron James de Rothschild, an early patron of photography, now an old man. Emulating the Bisson elegance was easy enough for Félix, who could summon a glittery crowd at a moment's notice. But was it wise? The Bisson brothers had gone bankrupt just like Le Gray: their plush boutique had thrived for a short spell, then all that good taste and luxury vanished.

Félix's legion of friends in the press stirred up plenty of excitement, and his famous friends did not desert him. Louis Thiriot, a young photographer from the provinces who came to Paris and joined the throng of Nadar acolytes at 35, boulevard des Capucines, was dazzled by the profusion of celebrities he saw there: Dumas, Offenbach, Doré, and the stars of whatever show now playing at the Comédie-Française. He was even more amazed by the fencing matches between poses: "There was always the fierce rattle of swords in the vast studio." Presiding in his inevitable red jacket (matching the red decor and announcing his political sympathies) was the artist himself, *le grand Nadar*, "universal" in Thiriot's starstruck eyes, "knowing everything and talking theology as well as history or mathematics." Thiriot was on hand at the studio for a legendary party during which Nadar asked Offenbach to play the *Marseillaise* on the piano. A rallying cry for the opposition, the song had been banned by Napoléon III; playing it with the win-

dows open to the busy boulevard was a potentially risky gesure. But Offenbach improvised brilliantly, concocting a version that fooled any imperial police who might have been listening and that delighted Nadar's republican pals.

On a Saturday night in March 1862, the carriages of fashionable Paris—and quite a few hansom cabs of the sort a man of letters might hire for the evening—drew up on the boulevard des Capucines, opposite number 35. A lavish costume ball was being held in Nadar's splendid studios. Charles Bataille, writing in *Le*

Boulevard at the end of the month, used the occasion to imagine a farce played out among Nadar's masked guests, one of whom waxes lyrical upon arrival: "Temple of laughter and games! Sanctuary where folly rings its little bells!" Félix, who could never disguise himself entirely—he was far too easy to spot—greatly enjoyed putting together outlandish outfits. He attended one ball dressed as a baby—a beanpole, redheaded baby with whiskers; for another, he transformed himself into the most unlikely Native American.

There was work to be done to sustain all this gaiety. Like his competitors, Félix advertised that he himself operated the camera (*opère lui-même*). Stamped on a finished print (in red, of course), the flamboyant *N* from the *Nadar* signature was intended as a guarantee of personal attention. But in practice Félix left day-to-day tasks to his manager and assistants; a hired cameraman could take care of routine portraits, freeing up the boss to concentrate on business affairs and the promotion of the studio. He had succumbed, as he knew he must, to the vogue for *cartes de visite*. If a customer strolled in off the boulevard and asked for a *carte* portrait, one of the assistants would operate a special camera that produced a negative with four images that could then be printed onto calling cards. Haphazardly—and too slowly, in the opinion of his investors—the rich inventory of Nadar celebrity portraits was being copied with a *cartes de visite* camera, an uninspiring job Félix naturally delegated to an underling.

Restlessness, the distraction of other interests, and his fondness for roaming the city and gabbing in cafés all contributed to his frequent absence from the studio, but so did the recognition that he couldn't—as his brother pointed out—do it on his own. To stay afloat, the business had to produce portraits on an industrial scale: dozens per day rather than two or three. In other words, it wasn't his personal charm or his faith in art or his quest for "intimate resemblance" that would make the difference.

THERE WAS A new look to the photographs that emerged from the new premises. In the glass box of the top floor, with its system of mechanized blinds and draperies, Felix could achieve subtle gradations of light and shadow—but only if he was physically present and only if his heart was in it. The up-to-date convenience of the new studio made it easy to turn out handsome, polished portraits likely to appeal to the crowds, but for the most part they were conventional images lacking the edge and daring and enigmatic beauty of his early work. Except, that is, when his interest was piqued, as it was on the day when a strikingly beautiful young actress came for a sitting. She was twenty at most and unknown at the time (though within a few decades she would

be the most famous woman in the world); her name was Sarah Bernhardt, and she made the old Nadar magic bloom again.

Loosely wrapped in a white burnoose, or in a shiny black velvet cloak, both garments voluminous, their folds teasingly suggestive, she leans on a truncated fluted column—a vulgar prop Nadar would have laughed at a decade earlier. It doesn't matter: the eyes are otherwise occupied, caressing her flawless skin, her calm pensive face, her untamed hair. It's not just that she appears to be naked under her wrap—the portraits carry an erotic charge that's complicated and enhanced by the withdrawn, private expression and a whisper of melancholy. The air of mystery is especially strong when she's wearing the black velvet and looking off to her right, almost in profile; the focus is slightly blurred, her bright eyes distant and enigmatic. Her sole ornament, a cameo earring, less a decoration than an echo in miniature, draws attention to her elfin ear, deliberately exposed and adding to the impression of nakedness.

Did Félix chatter away as usual while he adjusted her posture, the tilt of her head, making sure that the light fell just so on her

delicate face? Such was her talent—and his—that it seems impossible to imagine any voice intruding on her reverie. This was probably the first time she'd posed, but there's no sign that she needed his help, or anyone's, to feel at ease in front of the camera.

The fluted column, the cloak, and the burnoose all appear in other Nadar portraits, and Bernhardt herself reappears years later, in costume, celebrating her latest triumphant role, already a diva, already the Divine

Sarah. Here too she's giving a performance, but it's as naked as her slender body under the draped fabric: a young actress, vulnerable, alone, with something inside her—a fearsome ambition—that she's shielding from view, shielding from the celebrated photographer, tall, gangly, talkative, in constant motion around the studio.

If the photos of Sarah were serendipitous, not so the dozens of Nadar portraits of his great hero, George Sand, whom he and many others considered the most important living French writer, a passionate and rebellious heir of the Romantic age. Almost every aspect of Félix's life on the boulevard, from artistry to finance to family, can be traced through his close relationship with this woman who wrote under a man's name and was, at the time, his most famous client. Popular and prolific as a novelist and playwright, Sand had embarked (after the breakdown of an unhappy marriage) on a long series of romantic liaisons, usually with clever younger men such as Frédéric Chopin and Alfred de Musset, usually played out in the public eye. She liked to be seen dressed in men's clothing, smoking a cigar or a cigarette—more scandal. A writer of lesser talent would have had her literary reputation eclipsed by so much notoriety. But despite the disdain of some critics (Baudelaire, for one), her place in the pantheon of French writers was pretty much as Félix suggested in the *Panthéon-Nadar*, where she's represented as a noble bust on a pedestal at the head of the procession. Félix was enthusiastic about her politics as well as her prose: she was an outspoken proponent of women's rights, a republican, and a socialist.

The friendship began with Félix behaving badly. Sand had sat in 1852 for a portrait with a daguerreotypist named Pierre-Ambroise Richebourg, who had been one of Louis Daguerre's students. Richebourg's studio was a few steps from the Pont Neuf on the Île de la Cité, not far from Sand's Paris pied-à-terre in the Quartier Latin; convenience may have played a part in her choice of photographer. In any case, Richebourg's portraits were hideous, and Sand hated them.

She was forty-eight years old with a double chin, and the photos made both facts perfectly evident. Worse than the unflattering truth was the misrepresentation: she was neither anxious nor tired nor meek nor defeated—this "likeness" was the opposite of an in-

timate resemblance. Aghast, she ordered the negatives destroyed and stayed away from photographic studios for the next dozen years.

In 1861 Sand was put forward for a prize awarded by the Académie Française to the author of the "most honorable" literary work of the last ten years. Her name (and face) were suddenly everywhere in the press. Félix couldn't resist. He managed to get hold of a print of one of Richebourg's photos, retouched it, and sold it as a *carte de visite*—blatant piracy that reflects an urgent need for income in the months when the new studio was under construction.

The Nadar version of the Richebourg portrait is not a huge improvement. The double chin is less glaringly apparent; the folds on her blouse have been tidied up; and there's no trace of the piece of furniture she was sitting on—it's been blended into the neutral background. Her demeanor is less sad, but the portrait is still no good. When Sand saw it (friends and fans sent it to her, asking for an autograph), she repudiated it, claiming it was "apocryphal"—a photo of someone else made to look like her.

Yet she made no move to block the sale of the offending item. She and Félix had never met, but they had a history of friendly

mutual respect. He had courted her assiduously when he was assembling the *Panthéon-Nadar,* sending letters begging her to sit for
a sketch or at least to come see what he was up to; he let it be known
that a visit from her would mean more to him than all the visits he'd
received in the last couple of years. She demurred. *Quand j'étais
étudiant* (When I Was a Student), the collection of stories he published in 1856, two years after finishing the *Panthéon-Nadar,* was
dedicated to her: "To Madame Sand, with fervent enthusiasm and
profound respect." When he sent her a copy, she wrote back with
gracious praise (and a shrewd guess at his work habits), saying that
he had "lots and lots of talent" but had been in too much of a hurry
to finish his charming stories: they were too short. A few months
later, having completed the restoration of the small theater at her
château in Nohant, in the central province of Berry, Sand staged an
amateur production of a play "inspired" by one of the stories from
Quand j'étais étudiant. She also urged her beloved son Maurice to
have his portrait made *chez* Nadar, which he did.

The result is a plausible likeness of an elegant, diffident dilettante; mother and son were pleased.

In light of these cordial relations, Sand felt she had to find a tactful way to halt the sale of the "apocryphal" *carte de visite*. Having settled on a strategy, she wrote on September 18, 1863:

> *Dear Monsieur, you are selling a photograph of me that's making everyone scream and that I disavow as firmly as I can. If it wasn't being sold chez vous, I'd have protested a hundred times. But isn't the best remedy to make a better one? And for that, what must be done?*

Agreeing to the proposed remedy, Nadar invited her to the studio. Six months later she arrived for a preliminary visit to discuss her wardrobe. He promised that they would work on the portrait until it was a complete success. The next morning at eleven o'clock the first session began—and the day after that they started over again: another sixteen poses. All in all, four long visits were needed before the photographer was satisfied, by which time they were all fast friends: Félix and Sand, Sand and Ernestine (who acted as wardrobe assistant), even Sand and Paul, who had just turned eight and was, she declared, a "ravishing" boy.

On the afternoon of March 13, 1864, nine days after the first session, the three members of the Nadar family trooped in triumph over to Sand's Left Bank apartment bearing finished prints. That night she wrote in her diary: "Superb photographs."

She was right. Nadar knew exactly what he was looking for: the sense of a grand presence, calm and dignified, strong yet gentle, an implacable force for good. He had had her pose in three different dresses, standing, seated, in profile, looking straight at the camera and off to the side. Patient, tireless, he worked until he saw through the lens the woman he so admired. He wasn't hoping to disguise her age (she was about to turn sixty) or to recapture the slender and seductive young author who ruffled feathers with her cross-dressing and her very public amours. (But he did hire a specialist for the occasion who retouched the glass negatives, smoothing away some wrinkles and making the circles under her eyes less dark—a concession to her vanity Nadar would have preferred not to make.)

He was surely gratified by the praise bestowed a week or so later when an engraving "after the recent photograph of Nadar" was published in a popular illustrated newspaper: "This portrait renders admirably the nature of the beautiful head of Mme Sand, this vigorous visage where beauty mixes with majesty."

Other images were marked by a different kind of majesty: mock majesty. Giving way as usual to an antic impulse, Félix persuaded Sand to drape herself in the same velvet cloak worn by Bernhardt and to try on a Louis XIV wig he'd worn to a costume ball and kept in the studio just in case. The result was curiously satisfying and may have encouraged him to dress young Paul in exactly the same outfit. Were the two photos taken the same day? And was the photo of the child appreciated by the eminent author as good-natured satire? It's nice to think so.

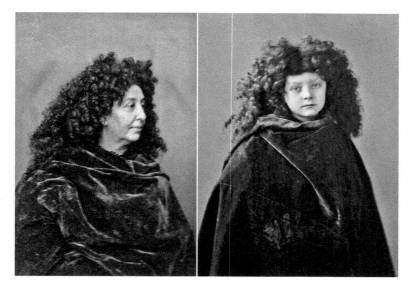

The portraits (with wig and without) were an immediate hit. They sold well in large format and also as *cartes de visite*. Soon Sand was complaining that she could no longer appear in public without being recognized.

The popularity of the portraits cemented the friendship. Their correspondence over the next few years brims with warm affection. Whenever Sand was staying at her Paris apartment, Félix and Ernestine would meet her for dinner, mostly at her favorite

restaurant, Magny, on the rue Contrescarpe-Dauphine (now the rue André-Mazet); Maurice and his wife would sometimes join them.

⸻ ✦ ⸻

THE FIXED COSTS Adrien had warned about were taking their toll. At the end of 1865, hoping to raise cash, Félix sold at auction part of his collection of paintings and objets d'art. When Sand heard about the sale, she wrote to express her concern—but a couple of months later they were all dining together at Magny. Félix reserved a loge at the theater where Offenbach's *Orpheus in the Underworld* was playing.

In the week before Christmas 1868, Sand sent Félix a short, typically sweet note ordering two hundred prints of two portraits in *carte de visite* format. She wanted them mailed to her in Nohant in time for the New Year. In reply, she received a long letter—undated, though clearly sent *after* the first of January—in which an apologetic Félix explained the technical constraints that made filling her order on time "more than impossible":

> Wintertime gives us gray, short days, and on some of those days we can make at best one print from a negative, sometimes

it takes two days to make that one print, almost always medio-
cre in that case, the paper having yellowed in the frame during
those thirty-six to forty-eight hours.

He managed to make eighty prints, he wrote, but wanted to
know before he sent them whether she still needed them now that
the holidays were over. If not, he could always offer them for sale
to the public, and they'd be gone by tomorrow: " 'You don't grow
moss on the shelf,' as we merchants like to say."

Next he proposed that she sit for a new series of portraits. He'd
had to spend more time taking care of the studio recently, so he
was confident he could make a better series—the old one no longer
satisfied him. (Sand had in the past kindly declared herself willing
to sit again—and repeatedly promised that she would never sit for
anyone else: "I've *faithfully* refused all other photographers, despite persistent offers.")

Félix's letter then took a darker turn, shadowed by the thought
of his debts. He hoped his financial situation would improve—and
if it did, it would be thanks to Ernestine. ("It is assuredly she who
will have saved the day.") His wife had been working until seven
or seven-thirty at night, slaving over the books, even though she
hated working with numbers. Then this remarkable passage:

> Without telling me anything, she found the only way in the
> world to make me recover my ardor and even my taste for this
> idiot job, so insipid at the end of 13 years of practice. She put
> herself to work from the first, without pushing or nagging me,
> and seeing her . . . valiantly dragging our heavy load . . . I said
> to myself, seeing her exhausted in the evening having exerted
> herself all day: — help her then to pull the thing!

The obvious way for him to help (as Ernestine reminded him
repeatedly) was to plant himself behind the camera and take photographs.

Sand's long, lyrical reply, dated January 24, 1869, is full of kind
wishes for the entire family.

Your wife will save you and in your turn you will save her, because the child must be saved and made into a man. Ah! if I had
money, I would bring you all happiness . . . ! I'll come see you
after the cold weather. It's so comfy here by the fire.

True to her word, at the end of April she arranged to have her
"old mug rephotographed" at 35, boulevard des Capucines, and
then a week later she returned for a second sitting—twelve more
poses. She wrote to Maurice with a cheerful update on the Nadar
family: they were "back on their feet," having sublet a part of their
house for twenty thousand francs a year and "watered down the
wine" (that is, lowered their sights). Félix wasn't allowing himself
to be distracted from his work at the studio, which was always full
and taking as much as twelve hundred francs a day. Thanks to Ernestine, they knew what they had, what they were doing, where
the money was going—they could even put a few pennies aside.
"Truly," Sand concluded, "that little wife has merit—if only he
had listened to her earlier." (Sand also remarked that Ernestine was
cleaner and well combed and working night and day—and that
husband and wife were "nice with each other.")

For one of the new portraits, Sand posed in an elaborate black
dress with a black lace shawl and a black lace mantilla, standing by
a fence post in front of a trompe l'oeil screen painted to resemble a
wooded landscape. She chose the costume, Félix chose the
backdrop—the two of them apparently conspiring to divert attention from her aging face. For another pose, seated on a fringed
chair that features in countless Nadar portraits, the background is
neutral, but the clothing is once again highly elaborate, the mantilla back on her head. Sand professed to be pleased with the portraits, but it's hard to imagine that the photographer felt the same.
Competent and conventional, they're fussy and faintly pompous
rather than majestic.

Sand is a forlorn presence in these photos—and the fact that
there's more to say about her outfit than her expression suggests
a sad decline in Nadar's ability to fashion a compelling portrait.
It was his final attempt to capture her likeness: when she returned
to the Nadar studio toward the end of 1874, an employee operated

the camera—the great Nadar was otherwise occupied. Sand sent a
mild reproof, saying she wasn't happy with the portraits that had
been made without him; she didn't want them to go on sale. But
though she offered to return in the spring, that reunion never took
place. She died in 1876, aged seventy-one.

What happened? It's not that his talent dissipated in the five
years between Sand's visits—well into his seventies, Nadar would
still be capable of taking great photographs. But he was rarely in-

spired to try. Even the presence in his studio of a preeminent author he admired without restraint was no longer enough to focus his restless energy. On the rue Saint-Lazare, photography had been "a marvelous discovery . . . that engages the most elevated intellects, an art that sharpens the wits of the wisest souls"; on the boulevard des Capucines, it was an "idiot job." In between those pronouncements, in the spring of 1866, Nadar declared that there was no such thing as "artistic photography":

> In photography, as everywhere, there are those who know how to see and others who don't even know how to look; there are those with taste, and there are boors, men of conscience who are merchants nonetheless, as in every trade.

He was afflicted with creeping disenchantment—but that's only part of the story. Other enthusiasms had seduced him.

IX

HIGH AND LOW

O N NOVEMBER 4, 1828, OR POSSIBLY 1829, WHEN FÉLIX was eight or nine, his parents took him along to see the crowds gathered on the Champs-Élysées for the Fête du Roi, King Charles X's saint's day. By tradition, the monarch fed his people on the Fête du Roi, distributing free bread, sausage, and wine—hence the crowds. Vivid details of the carnival atmosphere, a strong wind and swirling dust, the shouts of vendors and the murmur of the massed bodies, were imprinted on the young boy's memory by the trauma of what happened next. A confused clamor arose from the crowd as a shape he barely recognized as a balloon passed overhead, shaving the treetops, swept along by the powerful breeze. Dangling under the balloon was a little wicker basket, and in the basket was a human form, a man or a woman, clinging on. The apparition vanished as soon as he'd glimpsed it, chased by the wind and the excited crowd.

When it was gone, Félix felt his young heart horribly squeezed. "Poor devil," said his father, "he's probably already in pieces."

Although Félix never knew for certain what happened to the aeronaut, the scene remained for him one of impending catastrophe: the desperate balloonist in that puny basket hurtling over the trees' highest branches, only to smash against the roof tiles of a building in a street just out of sight. He replayed the events over and over in his mind, scaring himself with the seemingly inevitable crash.

From this persistent memory was born Félix's fascination with balloons—a fascination widely shared, given the novelty of these gas-filled flying machines. The first balloon to carry passengers was a hot-air balloon constructed by Joseph-Michel and Jacques-Étienne Montgolfier less than fifty years before the day of that windy Fête du Roi on the Champs-Élysées. Hydrogen balloons were invented immediately afterward, though for most of the nineteenth century balloons were usually inflated with a cheaper substance, the coal gas supplied by the municipality: the same gas that lit the boulevards sent the aeronauts aloft. At midcentury, tethered ascents at public gatherings still drew big crowds. One of the most famous early aeronauts, Eugène Godard, set up shop at the Hippodrome, a racecourse and fairground built in 1845 near the place de l'Étoile; he and his family sold balloon rides to members of the public brave enough to defy gravity and rich enough to afford a ticket at a hundred francs or more.

Félix's fixation was distinguished from the start by an urgent interest in the problem of how to steer an untethered, lighter-than-air balloon—that is, how to avoid the imagined fate of that aeronaut who had whisked over his eight- or nine-year-old head. Even before he made his first ascent (at the age of thirty-seven, at the Hippodrome, at the invitation of Eugène Godard's younger brother Louis), he'd become convinced that only something *heavier* than air—such as a bird—could navigate properly. He'd been only minutes in the basket, which had risen only a few yards, when he asked, "And you, do you believe in the possibility of steering your balloons?" Louis's succinct reply: "Never!"

This abstract concern in no way diminished his visceral joy in finding himself aloft: "And here I am up in the air, every pore delighting in this infinite sensual pleasure, unique to flight." Drifting high in the sky, for the first time he felt truly alive and blessed with a "superhuman serenity." (A serene Nadar! That's enough to convince us that flying is indeed a transformative experience.) Detached from the earthbound mass of humanity, he left behind all worry, every unhappy feeling. No bitterness, no disgust—even indifference vanished. Like the passage of time, altitude put petty terrestrial matters in perspective. From this highest vantage point, he wrote, one enjoyed an unobstructed view of Truth.

There was delight, too, in looking down on a patchwork world, an endless carpet, mostly green, on which a box of charming miniature toys had been spilled: toy houses, toy churches, even a toy train chugging along an invisible track.

After landing the first time, his only thought was to take off again at the next opportunity, which he sought out assiduously. Unwilling to pay cash for his rides, he offered his pen instead, placing in newspapers flattering accounts of the exploits of the "intrepid" Godard clan. Nadar's fame, combined with his willingness to promote theirs, made him a desirable passenger. Louis Godard and a younger brother, Jules, managed between them to turn him into an experienced aeronaut.

One evening in the countryside near Paris, about an hour after taking off from the Hippodrome with Jules, they saw a handsome property—wide lawns, fountains, women in white dresses on the steps of the house—and decided it was time to land. They drifted down to about sixty meters, and Jules waved and dropped his cap—to have the excuse of returning to fetch it. But just then a strong gust of wind swept them out of sight, and within minutes they were miles away. The wind was now a gale, dark cloud massing, daylight dwindling, and the fragile basket swinging like a pendulum beneath the balloon. They came down in the middle of a wood, the basket banging and bouncing as though it were on a spring, the anchor cable snapping. Jules kept yelling at Félix, urging him to hang on, but the latter, too inexperienced to be petrified, was instead excited to be risking his life in this terrible game. The whole rough ride lasted less than a quarter of an hour, the battering gradually subsiding as the gas escaped from the open valve, collapsing the balloon. The basket came to rest in a bush in a small clearing, where the passengers were greeted not by ladies in white dresses but by a shepherd's dog. It was midnight before they managed to find a horse and carriage to take them back to the city.

The next day Félix put an ad in the *Figaro* in an attempt to recover the lost cap—it was duly returned. And Jules recovered his balloon from the depths of the wood. He found it miraculously intact, surrounded by curious villagers. This fiasco, which might have served as a warning to Félix, had the opposite effect.

ALTHOUGH HE COULD hardly help wanting to photograph the astonishing spectacle beheld from the balloon's basket, the impulse wasn't primarily artistic or even aesthetic. His first thoughts were practical, commercial, entrepreneurial: he pondered the military applications of aerial photography, then the feasibility of conducting land surveys from on high. The possibility of making art rather than money out of the view from the heavens apparently never occurred to him. And yet with the promise of the attendant publicity surely spurring him on, he took up a self-imposed challenge: fancying himself part adventurer, part inventor, he resolved to become the first person ever to take a picture from the sky.

He chartered a balloon from the Godard clan and installed an aerial laboratory and darkroom in the basket. Then he and an assistant ascended to three hundred yards and operated the specially devised horizontal shutter on his vertically mounted camera with its Dallmayer lens. In the stuffy, cramped darkroom they slipped the glass plate into its chemical bath—and nothing happened. Astonished, they descended, prepared a second plate, reascended, and tried again. Nothing. Not the ghost of an image. They tried again and again with the same disheartening result. It was as though the lens refused to see the image, or the coating on the glass plate refused to receive it—an impossibility, unless some accident was hampering the process. He persisted.

The climax of the story is embellished with what looks suspiciously like novelistic touches. One evening in the fall of 1858, on the edge of the little village of Petit-Bicêtre in a quiet valley not far from Paris, he made another series of attempts and again failed. As the light faded, they landed next to a large apple tree. One of the Godard crew was about to deflate the balloon when Félix decided that he would give it one last try in the morning, so they left the balloon for the night moored to the apple tree, millstones in the basket for ballast. At dawn, on a cold, drizzly day, Félix emerged from the inn to find the balloon in a sorry state, the chill in the air having condensed the gas. To ascend, he would have to lighten the load.

He stripped out the laboratory, but the balloon barely budged. Stubborn, he decided to uncouple the basket: he would ride on the suspension hoop. Still too heavy. He undressed. Only his camera and the coated glass plate in its frame would go up with him. Perched naked on the cold metal of the suspension hoop, he rose to about eighty yards, peered down through the mist, opened and closed the lens, and shouted, "Descend!"

He threw on some clothes, hurried to develop the image in the relative comfort of the inn—and emerged triumphant. He'd done it at last: pale, blotchy, indistinct, but irrefutable, it was an aerial photo of the three humble buildings that make up Petit-Bicêtre.

With his success came the realization that the earlier failures had been caused by an unsuspected chemical interaction. During an ordinary ascent, the gas in the balloon expands as it rises, and some of it spews out of the appendix, the tubelike aperture at the bottom through which the balloon is inflated. Because on his last attempt his balloon had been insufficiently inflated, he had ascended with the appendix closed tight to conserve his meager supply of gas. Now he grasped that on his previous attempts, it was escaping gas interfering with the photochemical process that had prevented him from capturing an image: the gas had contaminated the plates and neutralized the silver iodide in the developing baths. That mystery solved, Félix's triumph was complete.

Playing pioneer pleased him. Back in Paris, he basked in the attention, showing off the proof of his triumph to all comers like a proud father with a newborn. When the novelty wore off, he moved on to a fresh challenge. Having experimented with electricity and magnesium flares in his portrait studio, he resolved to try using artificial lighting below ground, to become the first person to take a photograph in the complete absence of daylight.

His old taste for gothic thrills surely influenced his choice of the Paris catacombs as the venue for his first subterranean expedition. Disused quarries repurposed at the end of the eighteenth century to house the bones of millions of dead Parisians who had been buried in overcrowded, unsanitary cemeteries across the city, the catacombs were opened to the public four times a year. Visitors were required to apply in advance, and the tours were

generally well subscribed: several hundred sightseers, eager to behold stacks of bones and skulls and to contemplate man's common
fate, would gather at midday at the main entrance to this dank underworld, a little shack decorated with Doric columns aptly located on the corner of the rue d'Enfer ("Hell Street," now the rue
Denfert-Rochereau). A narrow, slippery staircase wound down to
damp vaults smoky from the lanterns carried by the visitors. Felix
wanted to make the ghoulish subterranean sights of the ossuary
available for perusal in the comfort of one's living room.

A few years later he embarked on a second underground project, again with the aim of revealing "the mysteries of the deepest
and most secret caverns." The venue this time was the Paris sewers, which were being expanded and renovated as part of Baron
Haussmann's modernization project. Eugène Belgrand, the engineer in charge, offered Nadar his full cooperation. A charming
drawing by the cartoonist Cham captured the bemusement of the
photographer's friends as he zigzagged between the heights and
depths of his enthusiasms. A bourgeois man in a top hat scans the
sky while a sewer worker in waders points to an open manhole and
says, "Looking for Mr. Nadar? He's not up there anymore! He's
down here!"

At a time when the technology for generating electricity was
still primitive, when batteries were both cumbersome and fragile,

the logistical challenge of taking photographs where no daylight could reach was considerable. Félix had to cope with what he called the "inconveniences" of the Bunsen battery, a metal and acid cocktail served in a large glass or ceramic jar, which produced less than two volts, emitted noxious fumes, and lost its charge as soon as the acids weakened. The dozens of Bunsen cells, wired in series, were too bulky to transport down certain narrow subterranean passages, so on occasion he had to leave some of the batteries up on the street and run leads down to his chosen location. Delays and malfunctions plagued both underground expeditions—"We're growing old here," an assistant was heard to mutter—but what better way to promote Nadar's patented system for photography by artificial illumination? The talent most conspicuously on display in his hundred-odd photos from the catacombs and the sewers is that of the master publicist. He was tapping into the public's fascination with the modernization of Paris and at the same time playing on nostalgia for the old Paris gradually disappearing as a result of the improvements above and below ground.

The catacombs presented an artistic as well as a technical challenge: how to convey the morbid thrill of an ossuary in a photograph. The idea of a catacomb should provide a delicious shiver of horror, yet what one sees in the old quarries below the rue d'Enfer is a storage facility, a rationalized system for warehousing skeletal remains. "Facades" of femurs and well-preserved skulls—a distinctly piratical arrangement—hold back and obscure vast piles of bones packed into the recesses of the cavern.

"The picturesque is quickly exhausted here," Félix noted. The glare of electric illumination, though it created dramatic contrasts, diminished the sense of mystery. But even torch-lit, tours of the catacombs were less than enthralling. "A few steps through these subterranean passages," he conceded, "is all it takes to satisfy your curiosity. It's one of those places where everyone wants to have been and no one will return."

He hoped to add drama by showing the process of sorting, carting, and stacking the bones—but here again he faced a problem. The exposure time when photographing with electric light in pitch-black conditions was about eighteen minutes, far too long to ask

anyone to hold a pose, especially if the idea was to depict live action. He came up with the ingenious idea of using mannequins. Seen
from behind, the figures are convincing. From the front, less so.

Looked at today, the photos are inadvertently comic. The ubiquitous skull-and-crossbones motif is neat and decorative rather
than macabre and menacing; the mannequins resemble a hokey
Halloween diorama. The horror of all those bones, whether loosely
jumbled or stacked in meticulous patterns, seems less pressing than
the need to get on with the drudgery of keeping the place tidy.

Félix did photograph one live human in the catacombs: himself.
He couldn't manage to hold his head still, so the face is slightly
blurred. He was probably trying to look nonchalant, ostentatiously

relaxed in the company of the disassembled dead. Instead he looks louche and a trifle irritated. His underground laboratory—the bottles with funnels poking out of them and open jars of chemicals scattered pell-mell—makes it look as though he were a sloppy worker introducing chaos into the somber order of the ossuary.

Because today we're used to everything being photographed all the time—we've seen the bottom of the deepest ocean, and we've seen earthrise from the moon—it's hard for us to conceive of how exciting it was to behold images of underground vistas for the first time. The photographs of the catacombs caused a sensation, as did the photographs of the sewers a few years later: catacomb-chic, then sewer-chic, swept the capital. Flaubert and the Goncourt brothers made a pilgrimage to the little temple on the rue d'Enfer. (Naturally, the ever-cynical Goncourts were disappointed with what they saw.) Small parties of bourgeois ladies and gentlemen took guided tours of the sewers—some of them led by Félix himself. An enthusiastic eyewitness account of such an outing begins, "All the newspapers have spoken of the enterprise of Nadar, who is photographing the sewers, just as he has already photographed the catacombs, with the help of electric light. What is less well known is that several pleasure excursions have been undertaken in subter-

ranean Paris by a certain number of people under the direction of the humoristic *littérateur*-photographer." Félix was riding a popular wave, a wave he'd helped bring into existence.

Despite the cost and difficulty of underground photography, he declared himself pleased with the fruit of his labor. He sent a set of the twenty-three sewer photographs to Belgrand, who immediately ordered a second set. Belgrand's enthusiasm is significant: what Nadar had captured was not the fetid black labyrinth famously described in Victor Hugo's *Les Misérables*—not the old sewers ("the intestines of Paris," Hugo called them), but the new, spacious, highly organized, highly efficient tunnels Belgrand had built. They were the belowground equivalent of Haussmann's boulevards. Visually arresting and aesthetically pleasing, Nadar's photos are conspicuously modern, some of them resembling abstract images of complex geometric shapes, some of them lingering on the means of their own production: carriages full of Bunsen batteries, jumbles of wires, and stands of electric lamps. The mannequins reappear, with similarly hokey results. But it's the emptiest images, the ones that look like illustrations from a modernist manifesto, that are most striking.

VISITS TO THE underworld in no way diminished Nadar's enthusiasm for the heavens. Squeezed between the catacombs in 1861 and the sewers in 1864 came his most notorious aerial adventure, aboard the monster balloon he called *Le Géant*.

It began innocently enough in early July 1863, with a morning visit from a fellow man of letters, Gabriel de La Landelle. This solemn, patient, methodical former sea captain (unlike Félix in almost every respect) came to the studio on the boulevard des Capucines neither to have his portrait taken nor to talk about books. (La Landelle had written several novels about the sea.) What he wanted was to talk about flight. More specifically, he wanted to harness Nadar's celebrity and promotional savvy to publicize a cause he cherished: aerial navigation by heavier-than-air machines. Obstinately dedicated, La Landelle had already written two books on the subject; his was the first use of the word *aviation*.

He had little trouble enlisting Félix, who was already preoccupied with the question of aerial navigation, as he explained in *Mémoires du Géant* with customary hyperbole:

> The idea I had been brooding on for so many years, to which I always returned amid the agitations, obligations, worries and even pleasures of a life already more full than necessary, this idea had taken hold of me, more and more my master every day. It seized me the way the Devil from Hell seized people in the Middle Ages:—having passed through Obsession, I arrived at Possession.

The possessed need no convincing. Clasping La Landelle's hand, he said, "We will march together."

A third character marched alongside them: Gustave de Ponton d'Amécourt, a rich, scholarly aristocrat prey to various enthusiasms (an archaeologist, he was the founder of the French numismatic society) who was convinced that the airscrew or propeller was the key to aerial navigation, that it would provide both lift and thrust. He coined the word *helicopter* and, with La Landelle's help, had built several prototypes—which could lift themselves into the air but came nowhere near achieving the aim of manned flight.

The first step was the establishment of the Société d'encouragement pour la locomotion aérienne au moyen d'appareils plus lourds que l'air (Society for the Promotion of Heavier-than-Air Locomotion), which met every Friday at Nadar's studio. Among the earliest members were Jacques Babinet, an eminent physicist adept at popularizing scientific advances; the philanthropist and arts impresario Baron Isidore Taylor; and Jules Verne, who six months earlier had published his first novel, *Five Weeks in a Balloon*. Félix, Babinet, and Taylor were honorary presidents of the society; Verne was given the title of *censeur*, which meant that he moderated the weekly discussions.

Félix, meanwhile, organized an event to trumpet the ideas of the fledgling society. He sent out several hundred invitations—"to pretty much everyone." On July 30 a huge crowd descended on the studio, filling it entirely and spilling down the stairs. He read out his recently composed manifesto, *Manifeste de l'autolocomotion aérienne* (Aerial Autolocomotion Manifesto); La Landelle and Ponton d'Amécourt offered a demonstration of their "embryonic" helicopters; La Landelle made a speech echoing Félix's manifesto and singing the virtues of the propeller; and a proponent of dirigible balloons was allowed to offer a rebuttal to the society's anti-aerostat ideas. Félix also announced the launch of an illustrated magazine, *L'Aéronaute*. The first issue, its banner designed by Doré, was published in August; four subsequent issues appeared at irregular intervals—but never attracted more than forty-two subscribers.

The failure of *L'Aéronaute* should not be taken as a sign of indifference on the part of the public or the press. Félix's manifesto excited a great deal of interest, with the reaction split between plaudits and derision. In this prolix document—all traces of his writer's block vanished when the subject was flight—he announced that aviation would erase national borders, eliminate distance, and make war impossible. He called for the end of ballooning: "The first necessity for aerial Autolocomotion is . . . to get rid of absolutely all kinds of aerostat." He proposed his alternative: "It's the propeller—*the sainted Propeller!* . . . —that will carry us into the air." And having specified in minute detail the mechanics of the "helicopter," he rallied the faithful with stirring rhetoric: "We owe something more to our century, the century of Steam, of Electricity, and of Photography:—we owe it aerial Autolocomotion." He closed on a note of humility that astutely measured his own contribution: "I submit the draft of this project to men of good will, and will count myself proud if all I have done is provoke a great Agitation in service of the cause."

The great agitation was amplified the next week when the manifesto appeared in *La Presse,* which had a circulation of more than fifty thousand. Félix also sent out copies to newspapers all around the world. "It was," he boasted, "like the beat of the tom-tom."

Sober reports on the weekly meetings at Nadar's studio popped up as far afield as *Scientific American.* And in its first issue of 1864, *Harper's Weekly* ran a full-page illustration of various "systems of sailing in the air," giving pride of place to Ponton d'Amécourt's helicopter—which the caption identifies as "Nadar's system."

In the accompanying article, Ponton d'Amécourt is mentioned in passing (his name misspelled); the tom-tom beat of publicity somehow reassigned credit for his invention:

Nadar's "Helicoptere" is composed of two screws placed horizontally on a vertical axis. When revolving, the wings strike the air obliquely, and send the machine up. For steering there is the third screw placed horizontally, with the axis perhaps oblique to those of the vertical screws. The motive power is furnished by a steam-engine specially designed for the purpose.

It's a wonder that Nadar's talent for promotion wasn't sufficient in itself to furnish "motive power" for liftoff. *Le Journal amusant* may have had something of the sort in mind when they put a satiric drawing of *"Nadaréostats"* on the cover of the issue published September 19, 1863. (The caricature is by Nadar's colleague and rival, Bertall.)

Making use of Nadar's promotional genius was always part of the plan. *Scientific American* reported that he was in the process of building a gigantic balloon. *What?* Why would a man dedicated to promoting heavier-than-air locomotion build a gigantic balloon—after calling for the abolition of *all* balloons? Because balloons draw crowds: the bigger the balloon, the bigger the crowd. Félix's idea was that the money raised by charging the public to witness the inflation and takeoff of a balloon "twenty times larger than the largest hitherto known" would fund the search for a practical motor to propel a helicopter, a motor powerful and light enough to allow for manned flight "in our first true aerolocomotive." A publicity stunt, *Le Géant*—"the last balloon," he liked to call it—was a strategic detour. As he put it, "Convinced of the impossibility of getting there by a straight line, I thought that a curved line could become, in the given case, the shortest path from one point to the other."

Construction of *Le Géant* began in August 1863 and was complete just a month later, the haste made necessary by a drastic shortage of funds. As Félix explained, any delay would have been fatal to the project: the balloon, designed with the help of Louis and Jules Godard, could pay for itself only by flying. Twenty-two thousand yards of silk were required for the vast envelope, which was in fact two envelopes, one inside the other, the extra layer intended to provide added security and the opportunity to fly higher and farther. The silk for each envelope had to be cut into 118 panels called gores, then sewn together, the work performed by an army of seamstresses stitching away in a rented dancehall.

In place of the cramped wicker basket that served as gondola on an ordinary balloon, *Le Géant* had a wicker cabin built on two levels with six separate compartments and room enough for twenty on the observation deck. It looked a little like a gingerbread house, with a front door and symmetrically positioned windows. In addition to a kitchen and a lavatory, there were bunk beds, a printing press, a darkroom, and a wine cellar. Félix was well prepared for a boy's adventure: he stowed weapons aboard in case he touched down among hostile natives. (Whatever complex reasons he had for building *Le Géant*, surely sheer childish fun played its part.)

Where to launch this fabulous creation? Félix's first idea was a racecourse. At the Hippodrome de Longchamp in the Bois de Boulogne, the gentlemen in charge refused the honor; at the newly built Hippodrome de Vincennes, they agreed but demanded an exorbitant fee. At last, thanks to the intercession of the playwright Victorien Sardou, who charmed a marshal of France, Félix was granted permission by the imperial army to use the Champ de Mars (the old parade ground where the Eiffel Tower now stands), an apt venue in that some of the earliest aeronauts had launched balloons there in 1783.

Fresh logistical nightmares presented themselves on a daily basis—none more pressing than the lack of ready cash. Félix spent virtually no time in his studio during the buildup to the October 4 launch: he was too busy running frantically all over town, wrangling with bureaucrats from the municipal gas company to lay a pipe to supply gas to the Champ de Mars, or pleading his cause with sympathetic bankers, or arguing with Louis Godard over technical design issues, especially the size of the *soupape,* the valve at the top of the balloon that could be opened to allow gas to escape. (Félix wanted it bigger; Louis balked.) When he wasn't focused on getting the balloon up into the air at the promised hour on the promised day, he was doubling down on that promise, publicizing the launch with all his considerable skill. His modest estimate was that four hundred thousand people, about a quarter of the city's population, would buy tickets at one franc apiece.

Less than half as many turned up on that overcast Sunday to watch *Le Géant* slowly inflate with more than two hundred thousand cubic feet of gas and reach its full height of nearly two hundred feet—about the same height as the towers of Notre-Dame. The crowd, though not of the predicted size, was still enormous; and liftoff, though an hour late, went smoothly. As he rose above the packed Champ de Mars, Félix looked down on the sea of upturned faces, searching with his binoculars for the two faces that meant most to him, those of his wife and child.

Another triumph for Nadar! His name, endlessly repeated by the excited multitudes, swelled the confused clamor of voices drifting upward to the passengers aloft in *Le Géant,* which sailed out

of earshot on a gentle breeze, about six hundred yards above the city. Defying superstition, Félix had insisted that the total number of passengers be thirteen. His brother, Adrien, was aboard (their feud in abeyance since their mother's death), and one woman: the pretty, fashionable Princesse de La Tour d'Auvergne, who had no experience of ballooning yet had demanded a place with aristocratic imperiousness. Félix was sufficiently confident to agree—but that confidence was not as complete as he would have liked. In the moments before launch, he allowed himself a stab of worry, imagining the balloon bursting, imagining it exploding, imagining that his obstinate dedication to the cause of heavier-than-air flight was about to end in a catastrophe fatal to himself and others. The blame would be his alone.

In fact, the flight went smoothly—for about three and a half hours. Though nominally the captain, Félix left the management of the balloon to the Godards and their assistant, Gabriel Yon, a master rope maker. It was a murky evening, then a dark night, nearly moonless, Félix's first experience of nighttime flying. Poor visibility added to the sense of disorientation. Unexpectedly, and with almost no warning, they landed, roughly, the wicker cabin smashing rudely to the ground, rising up, then crashing down with a thunderous jolt. The breeze was still light, but the huge balloon was a slave to every breath of air, and every movement of the balloon dragged the cabin along a terrain whose features they couldn't make out in the dark. The anchors proved useless; tipped over on its side, the cabin plowed along for a few more terrifying seconds, then came to rest.

Where were they? In a field about twenty-five miles east of Paris, near the town of Meaux, famous for its mustard and its Brie. Félix, who'd dreamed of reaching Russia, was bitterly disappointed by this unglamorous location. "A knockout blow," he called it. Once it was clear that no one had been injured other than his brother (a twisted knee), he turned to the Godard brothers, demanding to know why the flight had been cut short and why the descent had resembled a free fall. His words reveal his chief concern: "What can I say? We will be mocked."

But all publicity is good publicity. The ascent had earned thirty-six thousand francs—not what he'd hoped, not nearly enough to cover the costs, yet confirmation that people would pay to watch a giant balloon rise up and float away. He'd achieved, as he put it, "a semi-unsuccess." After repeatedly questioning the Godards about the precipitous descent near Meaux, he eventually learned about a serious malfunction: the valve had been wide open during the entire journey—which explained why Louis, Jules, and Yon had been busy shedding ballast throughout the flight, their activity increasingly urgent just before the sudden drop. Because *Le Géant* was so tall when inflated, the thick cord attached to the valve was heavy—so heavy that the valve opened of its own accord. The solution was to affix a lighter cord made of silk.

Aside from making that simple modification, Félix ignored the lessons of the frightening aborted end to *Le Géant*'s maiden voyage and announced a second flight for Sunday, October 18, again taking off at the Champ de Mars. Here his brilliance as a publicist again came into play: he asked the Godards to bring one of their normal-size balloons, *L'Aigle,* and inflate it next to *Le Géant*. Nadar's monster balloon at last looked the part. To prove its capacity, he arranged a couple of tethered ascents, with thirty-five artillery

soldiers loaded into *Le Géant*'s gondola—a dramatic flexing of the muscles.

As the crowd swelled, Félix was told—repeatedly, excitedly—that Napoléon III, the man he'd mocked so ruthlessly in his newspaper caricatures, had arrived to inspect *Le Géant,* accompanied by a guest, the young king of Greece. Perverse as ever, Félix allowed himself a long moment of republican petulance: he hid himself away in the service hut next to the balloon to avoid having to greet the emperor and his royal companion. Frantic friends tried to reason with him, but he refused to budge—until it occurred to him that in the press the story of his republican defiance might distract from the story of *Le Géant*'s launch. Nobly sacrificing his political principles to the cause of heavier-than-air flight, he emerged from his hiding place and said to his august visitors, *"Je suis M. Nadar."* A brief conversation about aerial navigation ensued. He then hurried aboard, a man on a mission, and gave the order to cast off. He heard the emperor call out, *"Bon voyage, Monsieur Nadar!"*

Among the nine passengers on the second flight was Ernestine, who had a strong premonition of disaster and insisted on accompanying her husband; her presence, she felt, would safeguard him. It was her first ascent in a balloon. The rest of the crew was slightly more experienced this time around: there were the Godard brothers and Gabriel Yon; two young men, Lucien Thirion, a writer, and Théobald Saint-Félix, a poet, both of whom had endured the rough landing at Meaux; Fernand Montgolfier, a very young descendant of the original aeronauts; and a journalist, Eugène d'Arnoult. Félix never mentioned d'Arnoult by name in his memoirs, presumably because the journalist had the temerity to give the newspapers a vivid account of his experiences aboard *Le Géant* (it was widely reprinted, as far afield as the *New York Times*) and then to publish a book-length account of the voyage, competition for Nadar's own *Mémoires du Géant*.

Again, the journey began peacefully, *Le Géant* shadowed by the smaller balloon, both drifting north from Paris. After a quick but jolly supper served on deck as night began to fall, Félix offered to relieve the Godards so they could get some rest. They declined, so he himself went below deck into his narrow cabin and lay down on a rubber mattress. Was he relaxed enough to sleep? He blamed unaccustomed noises—wicker squeaking under the footsteps of the passengers on the observation deck, ballast being poured through a tube on the side of the cabin near his window—for keeping him awake. He climbed back up the ladder to join the others.

They called out periodically when they saw lights below, hoping to find out where they were. (Anywhere but Meaux was the fervent wish.) Once, to their astonishment, they were answered from within a nearby cloud: it was the aeronauts aboard *L'Aigle,* which had drifted unseen to within earshot. At around seven-thirty they were hailed from the darkness below, a man calling out "Nadar!" Félix answered—it was his good friend the marquis du Lau d'Allemans, who happened to be staying at his hunting lodge near the forest of Compiègne, about thirty-five miles north of Paris. The marquis gave a blast on his hunting horn by way of farewell. Félix thought the encounter a happy omen.

Just before midnight they learned that they had crossed the border into Belgium; there was much rejoicing. The moon rose, and Felix asked the Godards to take the balloon up above the clouds so that the passengers on their maiden voyage (Ernestine, d'Arnoult, Montgolfier) might witness the weird splendor of a moonlit cloudscape. Only the urgent need to be certain of their location brought them back down: the constant worry was that a wind shift might push them out over the North Sea. The older Godard brother was especially concerned; on several occasions over the next few hours, as they drifted into Holland and closer to Germany, Louis urged that they land the balloon—advice Félix vigorously rejected, his principal argument being that landing in the dark had already proved perilous, his not-so-secret motive the desire to wipe out the humiliation of the first voyage by reaching Germany, say, or even Russia.

A stunning sunrise calmed their fears, but as the sun warmed the balloon and the gas inside began to dilate, they rose to above twelve thousand feet, which caused the gas to expand still more, stretching the double envelope of the balloon. Now Félix, too, was worried, afraid that it might burst. He asked Louis to valve gas and descend to a lower altitude, still hoping to continue the voyage. But Louis released more gas more rapidly than anyone expected. The descent was swift and alarming—alarming not merely because of the rate of fall but because closer to earth they saw that they were being swept along horizontally at high speed by a powerful wind. It was obvious to everyone that any landing would be hazardous in the extreme.

Even in ideal circumstances it would be difficult to land gently a gas balloon the size of *Le Géant:* there would have to be no wind at all, and the weight of the gondola would have to be in near-perfect equilibrium with the lifting power of the gas remaining in the envelope. The actual circumstances were dire: a tremendous gale and no way to keep the huge balloon from dragging them along the ground like a demonic amusement park ride. *Le Géant* was not equipped with a safety feature that had been designed as early as the 1830s for exactly this kind of emergency: a rip-panel that would peel open the envelope for rapid deflation the instant the gondola touched down.

"Hold tight!" The passengers grabbed with both hands the cables attaching the cabin to the suspension hoop. Félix positioned himself directly behind Ernestine in a corner of the observation deck, covering her body with his. Although d'Arnoult reported that during the dizzying descent Madame Nadar faced the inevi-

tability of a violent shock with "magnificent sang-froid," no one could remain unafraid in the ordeal that followed, a half-hour of terrifying mayhem.

Neither the large nor the small grapnel anchor was of any use; with the balloon traveling at nearly twenty-five miles per hour, even the thickest line would snap as soon as the anchor caught. Every time the wicker cabin smashed into the ground, it kicked back up again, rising as high as forty yards before crashing down with another bone-crunching shock. After several more thunderous crashes, they saw that the silk cord attached to the valve was swinging free between the suspension hoop and the collapsed bottom of the balloon's envelope. That meant that their grim situation was now hopeless: with the valve closed, the gas wouldn't vent, and their mad breakneck dance would continue until they were all battered to pieces.

No time to think about that disaster: train tracks ahead, and a train approaching on what would have been a collision course had not the alert conductor applied the brakes. Next obstacle: telegraph wires. Though the passengers avoided decapitation, the balloon ripped the telegraph poles out of the ground: they trailed behind like matchsticks.

In a moment of relative quiet, as the balloon skidded over a field of heather, it was decided that Jules would try to recover the valve cord by climbing out to the suspension hoop, a feat of gymnastic daring in the best of circumstances, foolhardy when the gondola was likely to bash again into the ground at any moment. On the third attempt, helped by Yon, he succeeded—but still the balloon careened on, like a "crazed comet," in Félix's memorable phrase, squeezing at one point between a redbrick house and an enormous tree, knocking down fences and kicking up muck from the barnyard, scattering terrified livestock. Shrubs and small trees announced the approach of a wooded area, and a series of deafening crashes signaled the beginning of the end.

Thirion was the first to be jettisoned, then Montgolfier and Saint-Félix; Yon and Jules were next, along with d'Arnoult. Louis Godard, left alone with Félix and Ernestine, shouted to Félix, urging him to tell his wife to jump out of the gondola, which had picked up speed again with only three passengers aboard. Louis was ejected, then the Nadars, on the far side of a wide stream. Félix was thrown onto the bank, while Ernestine was dragged a little farther to a stand of trees where the balloon's furious rampage ceased at last.

Memoires du Géant ends with Nadar crushed by remorse, weeping on the bank of the stream. Convinced that his beloved Ernestine had been killed, he had a vision of his son sternly accusing him: "What have you done with my mother?" D'Arnoult's version confirms that Félix's only thought was for Ernestine. He writes, "I saw on the other bank Nadar raise his head: he was very pale and appeared to be suffering a great deal. These were his first words on seeing me: 'My wife! Where is my wife?'"

The journey had begun with the emperor waving the balloonists on, wishing them bon voyage; it ended some sixteen hours later, more than four hundred miles away, deep into Germany, not far from Hanover, with their pummeled bodies strewn across the countryside, covered with blood and dirt. They were very lucky to be alive. Félix estimated that the wicker cabin smacked into the ground between sixty and eighty times in the twenty-five or thirty minutes of their ordeal. All of them were injured. The young poet Saint-Félix, who'd been dragged behind the gondola, was badly hurt, his entire body an open wound, one leg fractured. At first it was thought that Ernestine had sustained grave injuries, but when the blood and dirt were washed away, it became clear that she had a bad cut near her breastbone and bruising that was severe but not life threatening. Félix's legs were bruised and abraded; it was later determined that he had suffered a hairline fracture of the fibula in his right leg.

Woodcutters arrived on the scene. The injured were transferred to a nearby town and thence to Hanover, where the aeronauts were generously cared for by the royal family. The king, George V, took a lively interest in the events that had caused *Le Géant* to career across his kingdom. Félix summoned his seven-year-old son, who traveled by train with his nanny to see his battered parents. Sensational headlines appeared in newspapers all over the world, and soon thereafter came eyewitness reports: first d'Arnoult's, then Louis Godard's. Félix, on his bed of pain, began composing his own version, which was published in several French newspapers on November 7, accompanied by an illustration depicting the most dramatic moment of the ordeal: *Le Géant* heading for the train tracks, on a collision course with the locomotive.

The drawing (executed by Adrien) is a panorama from an elevated perspective. A graphic demonstration of the impossibility of navigating balloons, it marked the resumption of Nadar's campaign for heavier-than-air flight. Other popular illustrations focused on the human drama: the peril of the passengers and the chivalrous husband's attempts to shield his courageous wife.

LES VOYAGEURS DU BALLON *LE GÉANT* AU MOMENT DE LA DESCENTE EN HANOVRE. dessin de Nadar. — Page 397.

Nadar preferred the drawing he'd commissioned from his brother; he wanted to show the world implacable physical forces at work.

A less obstinate character than he might have given up on aerial adventures. Félix's moment of abject remorse passed quickly, however. Less than a month after the debacle in Hanover, taking advantage of the tremendous publicity he'd generated, he had *Le Géant* repaired and shipped it to London, where he put it on show at the Crystal Palace, sitting securely on the floor of the hall. *Le Géant* did fly again: in Brussels in 1864, in Amsterdam and Lyon in 1865. By this time even the infinite patience of Ernestine had worn out. He was on his way to the ascent in Lyon when she wrote to him with unconcealed emotion about the "damned balloon" that had separated them again after all the suffering it had caused. Would he ever give up his "perilous projects"? She had to say it: "Stop!"

Stubbornness was only part of what caused him to persist: he was now deeply in debt—120,000 francs by his estimate—and was too proud to raise money on his own behalf. Fund-raising had to be for a cause. There was also the matter of self-justification. The Hanover disaster was noble if Nadar was wholly dedicated to making human flight practicable; if he was merely a daredevil adventurer, however, then the disaster was a shameful scandal. As he put it in *Memoires du Géant*, "If it was a question of an act of folly, I'll let others say so, but a generous folly perhaps, and surely more than disinterested."

Some did indeed label it an act of folly, but many more rallied around to offer praise and even panegyrics. The physicist Babinet set the tone with a telegram: "The catastrophe of *Le Géant* is, to the letter, a public tragedy." George Sand agreed to write a preface for *Le Droit au vol*, a dogged polemic in favor of "heavier-than-air" flight that Nadar published a year after *Memoires du Géant*. (Privately, Sand agreed with Ernestine and begged him to give up balloons, go back to his studio, and take photographs.) Félix sent the manuscript of *Le Droit au vol* to Victor Hugo in Guernsey. The author composed a reply that began with "humble applause" and moved swiftly to a standing ovation and a rousing chorus of acclaim. After a fulsome tribute to the courage and audacity of the crew of *Le Géant*, he addressed the "magnificent transfiguration" that human flight would achieve. His rhetoric soaring into the stratosphere, he foresaw a "colossal pacifist revolution" and the liberation of humankind. Turning his attention back to Nadar, he wrote, "You've been accused of looking to make a noise. I have the idea that you're looking for glory. You could well find it." He compared Nadar to Voltaire and Christopher Columbus, two others who'd been looking to make a noise. "Your noise is good," Hugo concluded: thanks to the "racket" made by *Le Géant*, the question of how to fly had been "admirably" posed; "the solution obviously approaches." He ended grandly:

> Those who read this letter will perceive that it's to them that it's addressed. It's no longer to the aeronaut Nadar that I'm speaking. I have nothing to say that he doesn't know. I'm throwing this letter to the four winds with this address: to the whole world.

(After Hugo returned to Paris from his long self-imposed exile in the Channel Islands, he adopted an even grander way of addressing letters to Félix. He would write the word *Nadar* on the envelope, affix a stamp, and trust that any Parisian postman would know where to deliver it, even without an address.)

Writing soon after the "public tragedy," Jules Verne was only slightly more restrained than Hugo in his praise for Félix:

> First of all, this courageous and intrepid artist has revived the forgotten question. He has profited from his sympathetic position in the press and vis-à-vis journalists to focus the public's attention on this issue. At the beginning of great discoveries there is always a man of this caliber, a seeker after difficulties, enamored of the impossible, who tries, tries again, more or less succeeds, and in the end sets things in motion. Then the scientists get involved; they talk, they write, they calculate, and one fine day success breaks out for all to see.
>
> This is what Nadar's daring ascensions will bring: if the art of rising up in the air and steering through it ever becomes a practical means of locomotion, posterity, if it is just, will accord him a handsome part of the recognition.

Posterity was less generous than Verne had hoped. Nadar fantasized about a future in which civilization would be reshaped by aviation, but he played no part in the invention of modern aircraft. He did not foresee jet propulsion, and his monomaniacal insistence on the importance of the propeller meant that he had little interest in the aerodynamic qualities of wings. He did predict the ease of movement that aviation would bring: "From all corners of the world, man takes off, prompt like electricity, and soars and descends like a bird at the desired spot." Yet his powers of prophecy had their limit: he imagined aerial travel to be a pure delight, "no jolts, no noise, no dust, no fatigue, no danger." (Not in his wildest dreams could he imagine the dreary discomfort of flying on low-cost airlines.) He thought flight would abolish boundaries and armed conflict between nations, a utopian daydream mocked in retrospect by the hellish history of aerial bombardment.

DEBT FORCED HIM to sell *Le Géant,* and when he went up in it for the last time (in Paris, at the International Exposition of 1867), it was at the invitation of the new owners. After all the tireless activity devoted to the enterprise, not a penny was ever raised to fund research into heavier-than-air flight. The first manned "helicopter" did not take off until 1901; it was neither designed nor piloted by anyone connected with Nadar or La Landelle or Ponton d'Amécourt.

In a farcical reenactment of the painful legal tussle with Adrien, Félix became embroiled in lawsuits with the Godard brothers. They were after money (they claimed they were owed some eighteen thousand francs); Félix was after a judgment condemning their handling of *Le Géant.* Suit and countersuit, appeal and further appeal—the case dragged on for eighteen months and ended with a pyrrhic victory for Félix: the Godards were ordered to pay the legal costs; Félix was awarded damages of 272 francs and 10 centimes. Remembering Jules's heroics, Félix had the good grace to remark, "There are adversaries it is impossible to resent."

His fame had redoubled. He was mocked as reckless and acclaimed as dauntless. A satirical magazine plastered posters around the city announcing the "ascent of a man without balloon, without wings, without propeller, without mechanism, without cord, without balancing pole, and even without suspenders." About a year after Hanover, his loyal champion Verne wrote to announce that he'd modeled the hero of his new novel, a man with "the best and most audacious heart," on Nadar. The book was *From the Earth to the Moon;* the character, called Ardan (an anagram of Nadar), volunteers to fly to the moon in a projectile shot from a cannon. Verne's descriptions of Ardan—and even the illustrations in the first edition—make it plain that the novelist had studied Nadar closely, down to the chewed fingernails and the tufts of hair sprouting from the middle of his cheeks, and that he admired him immensely. Facetious, impatient, and combative, a big spender without a hint of avarice or greed, Ardan says *tu* to everyone, talks too much, always gets the last word, relishes practical jokes, and fights fiercely for lost causes. Above all, he's reflexively courageous—and carefree to the point of thoughtlessness. "Think!" he replies to a word of caution from a friend. "Do I have time to lose? I have the chance to take a trip to the moon, I'm seizing the opportunity, and that's that. I don't see how it merits much reflection." Both brave, both generous, Nadar and Ardan share an equivocal motto, *Quand même!* (literally, "All the same!"), which sums up their insouciant charm, their cheerful persistence in the face of adversity.

Verne's clear-eyed yet admiring appraisal of Nadar—the man he described as "enamored of the impossible"—seems to me both generous and accurate. The sad consequence of Félix's extracurricular activities in the 1860s is that all these frenetic adventures kept him away from the studio, the place where his true genius had flourished.

X

SIEGE BALLOONS

*L*E *GÉANT* WAS NOT THE LAST BALLOON, NOR EVEN Félix's last ballooning adventure. Three years after his final ascent in what Ernestine called that "damned balloon," when the Second Empire had collapsed and the Third Republic taken its place, Félix took to the skies again, this time in aid of his country.

In the summer of 1870, events were moving at a dizzying pace. In May the results of a national plebiscite had shown strong support for Napoléon III and his policies. Two months later a diplomatic crisis precipitated by the canny Prussian statesman Otto von Bismarck inflamed French patriotic sentiment. On July 19 France declared war. On August 2 the French emperor crossed the border into Germany at the head of his army. Bismarck later boasted of having provoked this aggression by waving a "red flag" in front of the "Gallic bull."

Despite his hatred of imperial rule, Félix leaped to attention at the outbreak of war. He and two other aeronauts, Jules Dufour and Camille Legrand (Dufour was known as Duruof, Legrand as Dartois—both nicknames bestowed by Nadar), formed the No. 1 Compagnie des aérostiers (No. 1 Balloonists' Company) and proposed to the military authorities that they make tethered ascents from Montmartre—they were volunteering to be the city's eyes. They drew up and signed a formal agreement putting Félix in charge, adopting military discipline, and disavowing any personal gain—this was all about honor and duty. They also proposed to manufacture new balloons. At the moment all they had to offer, other than their enthusiasm for aerial reconnaissance, were two tired old balloons, *Le Neptune* and *Le Strasbourg*, and some stationery printed with the grandiose name of their squadron. At work was the typical Nadar mix: disinterested devotion to a cause, boyish hijinks, and promotional brilliance.

The war, meanwhile, was going badly for France. On September 1, after a series of humbling military defeats, the battle of Sedan closed out any hope of victory: Louis-Napoléon surrendered and was taken captive. Three days later a Government of National Defense was formed in Paris. There were talks with the Prussians, but negotiations broke down when the new government proved stubbornly faithful to its pledge not to "yield an inch of its territory nor a stone of its fortresses." The young republic proceeded to declare war all over again, with the result that by mid-September, Prussian forces had laid siege to the capital, cutting it off from the rest of France.

Encircled, Paris was at the mercy of the enemy. A mere forty days had elapsed since the declaration of war; in two months Félix's beloved city—he had no doubt that the capital of France was also the center of human civilization—had gone from carefree City of Light to menaced prisoner of war.

Shocked by the scale and suddenness of the humiliation heaped on his country, Félix was nonetheless delighted by the demise of the "execrable" empire. Looking back on a lifetime of revolutions, he observed, "1830 had taken three days, 1848 three hours; in three seconds, the time to read the dispatch from Sedan . . . the Second Empire collapsed." Renewing their offer of assistance—but not bothering to wait for official sanction—he and his fellow *aérostiers* established within days a base of operations on the place Saint-Pierre, just west of where Sacré-Coeur now stands. The brand-new mayor of Montmartre—he'd taken office on September 5—was the future prime minister, Georges Clemenceau. At first he objected to the idea of a volunteer unit commandeering the place Saint-Pierre but soon changed his mind and even supplied the aeronauts with three tents and some bales of straw to keep them warm at night.

(Félix reported that the neighborhood's stray dogs were also useful in this regard: they made good natural foot warmers.)

The first tethered ascent was made on September 16, a few days before the Prussian encirclement of the city was complete. Day and night the aeronauts made observations, taking notes on maps of the Paris region printed up by Félix: red pencil for French troops, blue for Prussian, black for troops they couldn't identify. Up they went, four hundred feet above the city, as many as six times per day, equipped with compass, telescope, and binoculars, provisioned with a light meal and a jug of wine. When they came down, they dispatched their color-coded reports to General Louis Jules Trochu, president of the Government of National Defense—who never read them or in any case never acknowledged them. The unhappy fact was that Paris was now surrounded by an unbroken ring of blue.

Félix himself went up in *Le Neptune* both day and night. He left a brief, moving memoir of the many times when the wind was strong and he asked the National Guard for help with the maneuver, presenting himself to the sentry at midnight or in the early hours of the morning. Inside the makeshift barracks, the poor guardsmen slept on bare floorboards—no straw for them. He would choose fourteen or fifteen sturdy lads and wake them. Stretching and shivering, they would file out onto the place Saint-Pierre to do Félix's bidding. Their task was to man the cables in a vertical tug of war with the balloon: ten minutes for the ascent; ten minutes while Félix scanned the horizon, noting the location of Prussian campfires and checking that fire hadn't broken out in the city; and ten minutes for the descent. In all, the guardsmen braved the night chill for a good half-hour before they filed back to their barracks, without a grumble, expecting no thanks though the chore was not part of their regular duty.

BESIEGED AND BLOCKADED, starved of news and soon enough simply starved, the city suffered. The worst was that there was no way to tell the rest of the world what was happening. Nor could the authorities in Paris communicate with the provisional government, which had been established in Tours. Parisians who had family in the provinces were entirely cut off from their relatives. For a population accustomed to the telegraph and an efficient postal service, the enforced isolation was unbearable. Who knew how long it might last?

It was obvious to Félix that aerial reconnaissance was no longer the first priority; something else had to be done, something far more perilous. He proposed that the balloons be untethered, set free to float sacks of correspondence up over the besieging army in the general direction of the authorities in Tours. This time he was listened to, and the No. 1 Compagnie des aérostiers was at last in business—as postmen delivering the world's first airmail. The inaugural flight was manned by Duruof, who took off in *Le Neptune* on September 23, loaded with more than 250 pounds of mail and dispatches (about three thousand pieces of paper). The mission was risky, not least because *Le Neptune,* already well traveled before the war, was fragile and leaky after repeated observational ascents. Add to that the danger of falling into the hands of the Prussians, who threatened to shoot as a spy any captured balloonist. Taking off from the place Saint-Pierre at eight in the morning, Duruof wisely decided to shed large quantities of ballast right away, sending the balloon high enough to avoid angry musket shot. Three hours later he landed near Evreux, some fifty miles west of Paris, and by four o'clock in the afternoon he was in Tours, having traveled the rest of the way in a cart and then by rail. Among the items he delivered was a rousing, defiant speech addressed to the nation by the minister of the interior, Léon Gambetta, which was duly published the next morning in papers all over France.

Le Neptune also carried messages from Nadar. It's said that when Duruof was passing over enemy lines, he showered the troops below with Nadar's business cards, each one inscribed with compliments to the king and queen of Prussia—and to Bismarck. That story may be apocryphal, too typically Nadar to be true, but there's no doubt about the two open letters he wrote by candlelight in his tent just hours before Duruof's departure, one to a leading Belgian newspaper, the other to the *Times* in London.

The *Times* printed his letter on September 28, in French, under the headline "From a Balloon." This minor masterpiece of public relations begins by acknowledging the severity of the newspaper's past judgments on imperial France; Félix hastens to add that he, and others like him, were appalled by the "deplorable example" set by the Second Empire over the last twenty years. "I wish you could witness the spectacle," he writes, "of the sudden and unexpected transformation of Paris . . . utterly on its own, facing supreme danger. The city of pleasure, of noise, is serious and silent." He accepts that the initial blame for "this abominable war" lies with France, but argues that the failure of the peace talks has shifted the blame to Prussia ("the avid enemy, too sure of itself"), which is now waging war not on the French state but on the French people. "The older I get," he writes, "the more I've seen the eternal and ubiquitous practical demonstration of the axiom *'Tout se paie'!*" ("Everything is paid for," the rough equivalent of "What goes around comes around"). Today Nadar's compatriots are suffering; soon, he predicts, it will be the Prussians' turn. Without making a direct plea for British sympathy, he positions his countrymen as victims who've been "regenerated" by the trauma of national humiliation.

A huge propaganda coup, the flight of *Le Neptune* broke the blockade and lifted the spirits of the besieged Parisians. Victor Hugo supplied a rhetorically pleasing tribute: "Paris surrounded, Paris blockaded, Paris removed from the world, and yet with the help of this balloon, this bubble of air . . . despite the bayonets and the cannons, corresponding with the rest of the world." The only problem was that the correspondence was one-sided. As Félix put it, "Sending news from the inside was already something; the trick now was to receive news from the outside." Many schemes were proposed, including the obviously impractical notion of using balloons for the return journey. Imagine the scorn with which Nadar greeted the idea of steering a balloon past a hostile army to make a pinpoint landing inside a besieged city! He dismissed dirigible balloons as "flying fish." One pair of aeronauts in an ordinary gas balloon took off from Rouen, about seventy miles northwest of Paris, with the aim of landing in the capital; they abandoned their attempt the next day, when they landed in the middle of the Seine—but *west* of Rouen, some ten miles farther from their destination than where they had started. One far-fetched scheme involved floating hollow, hermetically sealed steel balls down the Seine; another envisaged suspending a high-altitude telegraph wire in the sky with balloons.

The most promising solution, already in use, was homing pigeons: the balloons flying out of Paris carried caged birds that flew back to the capital bearing urgent communications. But not every bird flew safely home—and of course there was a limit to the amount of information one pigeon could carry.

Or was there?

One evening in October, according to Nadar's suspiciously colorful account, a distinguished-looking man came to see him at home (he'd escaped the place Saint-Pierre to eat supper with his family) and proposed a scheme that left him dumbstruck with admiration. The man was an engineer with a sugar manufacturer and knew little about photography, but a theory had crossed his mind: in essence, microfilm. Gather the correspondence destined for Paris in a mail center in the provinces, photograph large quantities of missives, shrink the images, and send the microfilm to Paris by homing pigeon (affixing several copies to different birds, just to be sure). When one of the birds reaches its Paris roost, enlarge the microfilm, projecting it using a "megascope" magic lantern; clerks transcribe the writing on the wall, then the individual messages are sealed and delivered. Simple, elegant, and as it turned out, highly effective. Who was this distinguished-looking, wonderfully inventive engineer? Félix lost his business card and couldn't remember his name; he remains an anonymous hero.

First thing in the morning, Félix rushed around to see René Dagron, who'd been granted the first microfilm patent a decade earlier. Would Dagron be willing to fly to Tours in a balloon loaded with the necessary micrographic equipment? He would. Next stop, the government official in charge of the post office, who was "elated" by the plan and wanted Félix, too, to fly to Tours with a micrograph. Félix declined, explaining that he had no experience in micrography. (Besides, he was still hoping to be of use as an *aérostier,* still convinced that his chosen mission, aerial reconnaissance, was integral to the defense of the city.)

In truth, the government in Tours was aware of the potential of microfilm and had already used it successfully to send dispatches to the capital. But Dagron, who flew out of Paris on November 12 aboard *Le Niépce* (aptly named after Nicéphore Niépce, one of the inventors of photography) and made it to Tours after a fraught journey (complete with a crash landing and a narrow escape from Prussian troops), had perfected a rapid and efficient technique. Largely thanks to him, an astonishing number of missives were reproduced on microfilm and rolled into goose-quill tubes that were tied by waxed silk thread to the tail feathers of homing pigeons and sent to the besieged city—nearly a hundred thousand messages in all.

As Nadar wrote, "Our Paris, strangled by anxiety over its absent ones, breathed at last."

AERIAL RECONNAISSANCE did not bring Nadar glory, but his Compagnie des aérostiers kept him close to the action and assured him his place in the history of the Franco-Prussian War. Summoned one evening to a smoke-filled room in the ministry of the interior, he was sworn to secrecy: could he arrange to have Léon Gambetta, the most popular minister in the provisional government, flown out of the city so that he could rally the army and rescue Paris?

Nadar and his crew supplied for the occasion the first newly constructed balloons to fly during the siege. They were christened by Félix: *L'Armand Barbès,* after his republican hero who'd recently died in exile, and *Le George Sand,* after his good friend and literary hero. On the morning of October 7, the two balloons took off together, *L'Armand Barbès* carrying Gambetta and a colleague, cheered on by a crowd shouting *"Vive la République!"* as Gambetta waved his fur hat. Hanging from the basket of his balloon was the French tricolor, symbol of the nation's hopes for its young republic. The wind took them up over the top of Montmartre, then north over enemy lines. The Prussians greeted them with a salvo from their muskets and cannon fire from their vaunted Krupp guns, the bullets whistling around their heads, some even piercing the balloon. Having survived that encounter, *L'Armand Barbès* began inexplicably to lose altitude—it actually touched down briefly in a field where peasants warned the aeronauts that enemy troops were nearby. They heaved ballast out of the basket and climbed up to about seven hundred feet before gunfire again rang out beneath them. A bullet grazed Gambetta's hand. They rose up farther, out of range. A few hours later, when they finally decided it was safe to land, they missed their spot and crashed into the branches of an oak tree. Unsure about who would rescue them, Gambetta cried out *"Vive la République!"*—and the answer from below was *"Vive la France!"*

LIKE THE INAUGURAL flight of the airmail service and other similarly dramatic aerial episodes, Gambetta's hairbreadth escape became overnight the stuff of legend. The message he sent back to Paris the next day (by pigeon, naturally) boasted that the Government of National Defense was hailed on all sides, and the people of France were rising up. And yet the capital remained besieged. The success of the postal service—in all, sixty-six balloons flew out of Paris, nearly a third of them under the auspices of the Compagnie des aérostiers—boosted morale but not enough to dispel the gloom cast by the mere thought of an army of Prussians camped just beyond the city's fortifications. Parisians lived with this intolerable thought for four months, each month colder and hungrier than the last, before the inevitable surrender, which came on January 28.

Already by the end of October, Félix was thoroughly disillusioned with the provisional government, bitter about bureaucratic delays and the timid muddled thinking of the politicians, humiliated by mounting evidence of military incompetence, and outraged by the announcement that forty thousand francs were being spent to develop dirigible balloons—the despised "flying fish." Here at last was the republic he'd been dreaming of for decades, and still he found himself angrily opposed to the powers that be.

However, he never lost faith in his neighbors, his "admirable" fellow Parisians. He believed what he had written in the *Times* about the transformed citizenry of his beloved city. "Did it not seem," he asked, "that a generous breath of regeneration filled our lungs?" This, he claimed, was the hour of "supreme resurrection." More than a decade later he exhorted his countrymen to remember the spirit of those times, to remember the long dark nights, gaslights extinguished, when "Paris, the modern Babylon, was chaste." He boasted, on its behalf, of the safety of the city streets even at a time when policing was nonexistent, all the gendarmes having been conscripted into the army or serving as volunteers in the National Guard. Even the drunkards and the bums had vanished—or had they too been regenerated?

Félix reveled in solidarity, the new friendships made during the months of hardship, the old friendships cemented by devotion to a common cause. One new friend was Élisée Reclus, an eminent geographer, a vegetarian, and an outspoken anarchist. Ten years younger than Félix, he volunteered to help with the Compagnie des aérostiers and also served in the National Guard. In 1882, when Félix published *Sous l'incendie* (Under Fire), an eccentric memoir of the siege told in a medley of anecdotes and assorted prose pieces, he dedicated it to Reclus, in memory of the fraternal bond forged in those somber days.

The sudden death of the Second Empire meant that some of Félix's banished friends could at last return to France. Victor Hugo arrived in Paris, after two decades of self-imposed exile in Guernsey, at half-past nine in the evening on September 5, the day after the Third Republic was proclaimed, barely a week before the capital was encircled. He was welcomed home by a jubilant crowd who serenaded him with the *Marseillaise* and demanded that he address them, which he did—four times.

Even before Félix enlisted Hugo in the cause of heavier-than-air aero-locomotion, the photographer and the eminent author had recognized each other as kindred spirits, with similarly radical political postures and a similar taste for self-promotion. ("What I write doesn't belong to me," Hugo concluded late in life. "I am public property.") Félix, along with a horde of writers and journalists, had been invited in September 1862 to the famous Banquet des Misérables, a grand dinner party organized in Brussels by Hugo's publishers to celebrate the astonishing success of Hugo's *Les Misérables*. Having traveled to Belgium with his old bohemian pals Carjat and Banville, Félix returned laden with tracts by Hugo that were banned in France, among them *Napoléon le Petit*, a stinging denunciation of the emperor, and copies of the unexpurgated edition of *Les Châtiments*, a collection of satirical poems attacking the corruption and decadence of the Second Empire.

Back from exile, Hugo composed three appeals aimed respectively at the Germans, the French, and the Parisians. He addressed the Germans as a friend, he said, warning them of the folly of trying to take Paris by force. As for his compatriots, he urged them to rise up and resist the invading army. Eager to see these messages distributed as widely as possible, Félix arranged to have the pamphlets used as ballast, instructing his aeronauts to toss out a half-dozen pounds' worth at a time as they passed over enemy lines. When the moment came to christen the fifth balloon manufactured by the Compagnie des aérostiers, Félix made the obvious choice: *Le Victor Hugo*. It took off on October 18 carrying nearly a thousand pounds of mail and six homing pigeons. In among the correspondence was a private letter from Hugo destined for London. To Félix he wrote, "I couldn't ask for more than to be raised up into the sky by you. Thank you from the bottom of my heart."

———

THE NOTEBOOK HUGO kept at the time, recording the visits paid by Nadar among many others, provides a clear-eyed and empathetic glimpse of privileged Parisian life during the siege.

On October 8—the day he receives his first letter from outside Paris since the imposition of the blockade—he notes that the supply of sugar in the city is dwindling and that meat rationing has begun. A week later there's no more butter, no more cheese, hardly any milk or eggs. Soon the only meat Parisians are eating is horsemeat. Or rats, which cost forty cents apiece. By the end of November, rat pâté has become a standard dish; Hugo is told it tastes good. A friend brings him a haunch of antelope from the zoo at the Jardin des Plantes—it's delicious. On December 1 he eats bear, also from the zoo, but makes no comment on the flavor.

In the distance, cannon fire reminds them that their plight could worsen. Sometimes the guns can be heard all night. A cold snap freezes the Seine. Just before Christmas, Hugo enjoys a lively dinner with friends, despite the deprivations and the ever-present menace. He considers the possibility that if Paris is taken, he'll be arrested and imprisoned in a German fortress. "After Guernsey, Spandau. So be it."

Théophile Gautier comes to him for help. Gautier has a horse, and the horse has been requisitioned. Would Hugo intercede to keep the horse from being butchered and eaten? Hugo speaks with the relevant authorities. The horse is spared.

At the end of December, Hugo writes, "It's not even horse we're eating. Maybe dog? Maybe rat? I'm beginning to have stomachaches. We're eating the unknown."

New Year's Day: "I'm hungry. I'm cold. Just as well. I suffer what the people suffer."

In early January, the Prussians began to bombard the city with siege guns, a barrage that lasted twenty-three days and caused more damage to Paris than any previous or subsequent attack. Capitulation, on January 28, 1871, was followed three weeks later by a victory parade by the Prussian army through the streets of the city. The humiliation of the French was complete.

Surrender meant the blockade was over, but that relief lasted only a few months. Having suffered at the hands of the Prussians, the Parisians now embarked on that bloody cycle of self-inflicted suffering known as the Commune, in essence a French civil war waged in and around the capital for two merciless months. Though Nadar admired the ideals of the Communards and by now thoroughly despised the Third Republic, he saw clearly that the leaders of the Commune were ushering in a further catastrophe at a moment when the country's endurance was exhausted. He stayed prudently out of sight while the municipal government and the national government (now located in Versailles) fought each other with a senseless savagery that surprised everyone. As Hugo wrote in the midst of the tragedy, "This Commune is as idiotic as the National Assembly is ferocious. From both sides, folly." The conflict became a second siege, the army loyal to the National Assembly pinning the National Guard units loyal to the Commune inside the city walls. The Communards were eventually defeated in late May, in what's known as the Bloody Week, an horrific episode marked by summary executions, arson, and outright massacre. Some ten thousand Communards are thought to have died in the fighting.

Looking back on the war and the Commune, Félix, not surprisingly, laid the blame for the latter on the former—in short, he blamed Louis-Napoléon and the Second Empire for setting the scene. "The history of the siege," he wrote, "the *true* history . . . has not yet been written and can't be yet, nor that of the second siege, which was the immediate, ineluctable consequence . . . of the first. The two histories will be written one day, when fresh air has chased away the odor of betrayal and the bloody fog."

He wrote little about the Commune, most likely because it

shamed him, casting his city and his fellow citizens in a deeply unpleasant light. A brief memoir, soberly entitled *Deposition,* explains his attitude toward the conflict without ever mentioning the political crosscurrents of the whole appalling affair. The time is late March 1871, soon after the Commune routed the army from the capital; the place is his apartment. He's been sick for two long months, so sick that the doctors fear for his life. A noise from the boulevard draws the entire household to the windows; he follows (and soon regrets the "unhealthy contagion of curiosity"). Coming down the boulevard they see an incalculably long column of prisoners, marching four abreast, many of them clearly young army soldiers, but also others of all kinds, in every kind of outfit and uniform, guarded by mounted soldiers of the National Guard. The prisoners, all male, all detained by the Commune, have not been condemned or judged or even interrogated; they are simply being shifted from one guarded barracks to another. Surging around them is a loud and bloodthirsty crowd clamoring for their death, insisting at the top of their lungs that each and every prisoner be put to death right away, right here, right now—massacred in the street. One falsetto voice cries out more stridently than the others, a woman who screams, "Pull out their fingernails!"

The last paragraph of the memoir reads,

Yes, that's what I saw and heard right in the center of Paris, the center of Human Civilization,—and in sincere witness, disinterested, with all other testimony concurring . . . as it's my duty, I submit my deposition.

XI

A LONG GOOD-BYE

FTER THE WAR, AFTER THE COMMUNE, ORDINARY things began to happen to our extraordinary hero, as though a spell had worn off, a spell that had set him apart and made him bigger, brighter, busier, more foolish, daring, stubborn, and lovable than anyone around him. He was still capable of springing surprises, and his genius as a portraitist never deserted him—he was still *le grand Nadar*—but his optimism, his cheerfulness wavered. He turned fifty just before the war, and for the first time began to comment on his age; aches and pains (kidney trouble) and illness, to which he'd been immune, now nagged him. He remained unusually energetic even as an old man, but his confidence in the result of his exertions had ebbed. He was no longer superhuman.

And yet . . . one more tale of derring-do. In the immediate aftermath of the Commune, the government was eager to prosecute and punish anyone connected with the insurrection. Although there were rumors that he himself would be arrested, if only because he was a notorious radical, Félix took the risky decision to shelter anyone who appealed for his help and to lend vocal support to friends such as Élisée Reclus who were put on trial. Among those he hid and helped to escape France were Félix Pyat, a journalist who played a bloody, destructive role in the Commune, and Jules Bergeret, a captain in the National Guard who rose in those tumultuous months to the rank of general. Both men were tried in absentia by the Versailles government, and death sentences were handed down—in other words, Félix's generosity may well have spared their lives. This was a principled generosity: though he'd known Pyat for decades, he felt only mild sympathy for him, and he barely knew Bergeret at all.

According to Félix, the sound of summary executions was still echoing in the streets when a woman came to see him and handed him a note that read, "I am lost, save my wife"—it was signed Bergeret. Félix asked the woman if she knew the couple in question, and she replied that she was hiding them in her apartment, but her neighborhood was full of soldiers. Félix said the general and his wife should come to his house that evening, which they did. They spent the next thirteen days *chez* Nadar, the entire household in a state of extreme anxiety, dreading arrest.

Desperate to put an end to the danger, Félix set in motion a bold plan. He wrote to Alexandre Dumas *fils*, who was both famous (as the author of *The Lady of the Camellias*) and impeccably conservative, and suggested that the two of them go to Versailles and talk to the head of the government, Adolphe Thiers. Dumas agreed—though he said that if he had Bergeret in his apartment, he'd strangle him. The two celebrities (one radical, one reactionary) met with Thiers, who took one look at Nadar and professed amazement that he hadn't been shot yet. His reaction to the news that Nadar was harboring General Bergeret was furious: "Why the devil have you come to tell me this?"

Nadar explained that he was not looking for a passport for Bergeret or even safe-conduct. Instead he proposed that the three of them pick one of their friends in common, someone reliable, and Thiers would send that person on a foreign mission, along with his secretary—and the secretary would be Bergeret, traveling under an assumed name. No one else need ever know about it.

Félix wrote, "I was so intent on achieving the desired result that my will prevailed." But sheer audacity and the masterstroke of enlisting Dumas had as much to do with his success as willpower. He waited to tell this story in print until 1894, fourteen years after the government issued a blanket amnesty to the Communards, seventeen years after the death of Thiers. As for Bergeret, he settled in London, then moved to New York, where he died after the turn of the century, age seventy-five; his letters to Félix were filled with gratitude.

A COMMERCIAL DISASTER for nearly every business in Paris, the war forced Félix to scale back. He closed down the studio on the boulevard des Capucines and rented a smaller establishment at 51, rue d'Anjou. It was not much more than a twelve-minute walk between the two places, but in other respects the difference was vast: no more indoor waterfalls, no more fifty-foot gaslit signs on the facade.

The interior of the new premises was elegant and well appointed, the ubiquitous red giving way to pink.

By Félix's estimate, he was two hundred thousand francs in debt when he set up the new studio; his operating capital was 250 francs in cash. Ernestine took charge, welcoming clients, taking their money, keeping the accounts in good order. She had the future in mind—not hers, not her husband's, but their son's. Paul was a teenager now, sensitive, dreamy, whimsical. Working with his father and the studio assistants, he was quick to learn the trade. After returning from his military service in 1876, he became artistic director of the studio; he was barely twenty, a dashing young dandy complete with waxed mustache.

⸻❖⸻

BY THE END of the decade, Félix had in effect withdrawn from the business, which now employed two dozen people, mostly catered to the rich, and produced a sought-after commercial product that bore little resemblance to the austere magnificence of the rue Saint-Lazare portraits. By the mid-1880s, after more than a decade of hard work, Félix and Ernestine were solvent again—and Paul was wholly responsible for day-to-day operations.

Félix peered through a camera lens when it suited him, or when an old friend wanted a portrait made. As always, his fame helped attract clients, and he also offered Paul advice, encouragement, and occasionally criticism. Unlike the failed partnership with his brother, this one worked: in the early days, professional collaboration between father and son was fruitful and relatively frictionless.

Baron Taylor showed up at the rue d'Anjou soon after the new studio opened, and the Nadar portrait made that day is as fine as

anything produced on the rue Saint-Lazare. Taylor's unfailing generosity was an anchor in uncertain times, not only for Félix but for countless artists and writers. Boldly lit, massive, and immovable, he's a monument to the fixed purpose of dedicated philanthropy.

When Victor Hugo came to have his portrait taken in 1878, Félix was on hand for the session, working side by side with Paul. Afterward Hugo wrote to Félix expressing his gratitude: "I've received the superb prints. . . . You succeed in everything. Even with an old noggin like mine." Topped with white wispy hair, and framed by a gnarled beard that seems to start above the ears (concealing them entirely) and truss up the chin, the old noggin is a noble patriarch's badge of honor, a testament to endurance. The seventy-six-year-old author, newly elected to the Senate, wears his hard-won wisdom and the weight of the years—his load of triumph and tragedy—with patient fortitude. He is a national treasure, but there's no trace of pride in his features. The photographs are at once loving and unforgiving, drawing our attention to the sharp nail on his little finger, the fragile veins standing out on the broad expanse of his famous forehead, and the swollen pouches beneath eyes that have seen too much.

The friendship between the two men had deepened. When the author invited the photographer to dinner one evening in the summer of 1876, he specified that it would be a family supper—and that Félix was one of the family. So it's not surprising that Hugo thanked the father for the photos, even though the son may have done much of the work.

Hugo died of pneumonia in the early afternoon of May 22, 1885. His daughter-in-law sent a note that evening to the rue d'Anjou, and Félix and Paul came the next morning. The commemorative photo they took, delicate and dramatic, tender and pitiless, was published as an engraving on the front page of *L'Illustration*, a popular weekly, and sold in large quantities from the studio.

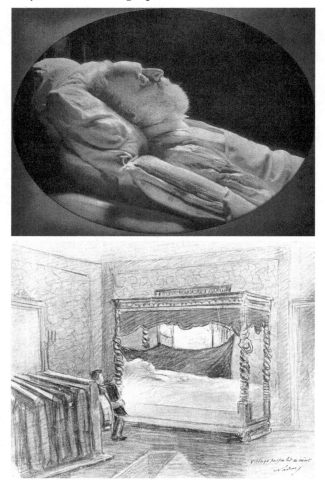

Perhaps sensing that he and Paul were at work on a masterpiece of postmortem photography, Félix sketched the deathbed scene in a way that reveals how the image was achieved, the camera lens in the foreground, the black cloth strung up behind the corpse to provide contrast, an assistant (probably Paul) holding a reflector to catch the bright May daylight from the open window.

A little more than a year later, toward the end of the summer of 1886, Paul made a suggestion that led to Nadar's last photographic triumph: he urged his father to interview the eminent scientist Eugène Chevreul, who was about to celebrate his hundredth birthday. Chevreul's work as a chemist had led to practical improvements in basic necessities such as soap and candles; his work with color and his "chromatic diagrams" had significant influence on the arts. Here was a scientist whose research had a measurable impact on people's lives—and he'd been born in the eighteenth century, before the French Revolution. Grasping at once the significance of the project, delighted by the chance to interact with a celebrated man of science, Nadar launched himself into photojournalism, a leap made possible by advancements in the photographic process (rapid exposure time now allowed for unposed "instant" snapshots) and by photogravure. Félix interviewed Chevreul over the course of three days, during which Paul took fifty-eight photos. Félix then edited the interview, selected a dozen images, and captioned them with the centenarian's words.

If the result—which caused a sensation when published a week later under the title "The Art of Living a Hundred Years"—looks strikingly familiar, that's because he'd set a pattern for newspapers and magazines that persists to this day.

Félix was well aware of what he was up to. "For the first time," he wrote, "the reader will effectively be a spectator, as though he were taking part." The fact of the matter is that he'd radically condensed the interview and, for dramatic effect, rearranged the order of Chevreul's remarks; a spectator, in other words, would have experienced something rather different. The last image in the series shows the scientist with his mouth open, speaking forcefully, gesturing for emphasis.

12. « — Je ne vous ai pas tout dit. Mais il ne suffit pas de dire : il faut prouver, il faut faire *voir!* Il faut que je vous fasse *voir!* Il faut que vous *voyiez! Je veux faire voir, parce que c'est quand je vois, que je crois!!! »

The caption reads, "—I have not told you everything. But saying is not sufficient: One has to prove, one has to *show*! I have to make you *see*! You have to *see*! *I want to show, because it's when I see that I* believe!!!" The perfect synergy of Chevreul's repeated insistence on ocular proof and the image that purports to show him saying those exact words conceals a sharp irony: Félix matched caption and image without regard for the topic at the moment the photo was taken. There's no knowing what gesture Chevreul was actually making when he said "One has to prove, one has to *show*!"—no way of telling what expression was on his face. Like many of Nadar's remarkable achievements, this one is profoundly equivocal: he fudged the truth to insist—in all sincerity—on the importance of both verifiable reporting and scientific proof.

And then moved on: his first photo interview was his last.

Photography no longer held his interest. Already in 1882, when a prospective client wrote saying he wanted a portrait of his wife, the photographer replied that he was no longer at the studio, "having more than lost my touch in the three years since Paul Nadar relieved his father."

WHAT WAS FÉLIX up to? Scribbling, mostly. In the years between his fifty-seventh birthday and his eightieth, he published five collections of miscellaneous writing—anecdotes, elaborate jokes, political harangues, biographical sketches, philosophical musings, prose poems—most previously published in newspapers or magazines, all jumbled together. Each of the books has a loose, sometimes very loose, organizing principle, but none is entirely coherent. They're all entertaining, and they all have flashes of brilliance (and tedious passages, too). None of them had any great popular success when first published, and today, sadly, nobody reads them at all. Topical material makes up the bulk of several of the volumes—commentary on politics, local quarrels, and other ephemera, news items that stopped being news back in the nineteenth century.

Félix was still spending many days at the rue d'Anjou studio—and possibly wishing he could play hooky more often—in 1877, when he published *Histoires buissonnières* (Truant Tales), the first

and most literary of his later books. Each of the twenty-four dis-
crete chapters is dedicated to a friend, as though he had written
them solely to give pleasure to his pals. One chapter, "To a Young
Writer," dedicated to Édouard Manet (who was neither young nor
a writer and therefore unlikely to take offense), is a relentlessly sar-
castic litany of advice, an antimanifesto that reveals, when turned
inside out, what Félix truly believed about the discipline he now
preferred to photography. "Above all," he counsels, "be serious
and fear Ideas." Self-seriousness is a cardinal virtue, he explains: if
you have it, you don't even need to know how to spell. As for ideas,
they all contain something shocking, and your first duty is to avoid
shocking anyone. "Smile, if you wish, and sniff sadly if you must;
but don't laugh or cry, and—crucially!—never get angry! No
noise, no éclat." He recommended a "flowing, mellifluous" style:
unctuous, spineless, moderate, colorless.

Already in *Mémoires du Géant* he had perfected the opposite,
a rattling, headlong journalistic prose style, less like written than
spoken French, proud of its rough energy and unafraid to shout
out, jump around, and gesture rudely. Polemic was his natural
bent, especially where politics and social injustice were concerned.
As a writer, he wanted to grab you and shake you hard, to breathe
in your face. To be indecorous and unconventional was for him a
sign of authenticity. This is not to suggest that his writing was artless or unskilled; on the contrary, in his second incarnation as a
writer, he was a disciplined craftsman who worked to give his prose
the irrepressible vitality he displayed in person. More often than
not, he succeeded; he charmed (or irritated) his reader as he would
a chance acquaintance accosted in a café.

Théodore de Banville, by now a venerated poet, wrote the preface to *L'Hôtellerie des coquecigrues* (The Mythical Beasts' Hotel),
and though under the circumstances Banville could hardly be im-
partial about his old friend's book, he succeeded in capturing its
quintessentially modern quality:

> Here, reader, is a very original book, brief, rapid, incisive, as
> they must be to be read, in this age that's at once furious and
> somnolent, by people who have time neither to live nor to die.

Our time isn't precious, but it's rare, to the point where the supreme politeness, in town and even on stage, consists in never unleashing a tirade.

He argues that Nadar's book is fearless because it resembles its fearless author:

> The civilized fellow who wrote these random notes with a pencil stub found in his pocket is horrified by trite platitudes, as though he were a savage, and maybe he deserved to have been born in a savage country. And yet he's Parisian to the tip of his fingernails, and there's not an inch of asphalt on the boulevard that hasn't met the sole of his boots.

He insists on his friend's bravery (he "boldly calls a cat: a cat, and if need be: two cats"); his indifference to financial gain ("I've known Nadar forever; I've seen him rich, thanks to his work, to his indefatigable ardor, and I don't know any man less impressed with money than him"); his willingness to stick his nose in other people's business; and his wit, which Banville claims is compounded of good humor and indignation.

Invoking Nadar's multitude of friends (but naming only Baudelaire, who'd been dead ten years), Banville presents the author of *L'Hôtellerie des coquecigrues* as "a good and frank companion." Again he's hit on an essential quality of Nadar's late writing: his eagerness to be in cahoots with the reader, to force a meeting of the minds (even while spouting contentious opinions). Addressing the reader in a coda to *Histoires buissonnières*, Nadar says with direct simplicity that he wants to remain friendly after parting company on the final page. "I have for you the affection of a brother," he writes, "and I want to leave you with fond memories.—Goodbye!" An envoi is a common literary convention, but Nadar gives it the illusion of a heartfelt personal farewell.

L'Hôtellerie des coquecigrues was published in 1880, and a very similar volume, *Le Monde où on patauge* (The World We're Mired In), came out three years later. In between, in 1882, came *Sous l'incendie*, a book with a brooding retrospective slant—a mulling-over of events and personalities associated with the disaster of the Franco-Prussian War and its aftermath—interspersed with a few seemingly random vignettes.

In 1900, the year he turned eighty, Nadar published *Quand j'étais photographe* (When I Was a Photographer), a canny, elliptical, often intemperate pseudo-memoir that gives away very little about his actual experience behind a camera. Though he includes a few entertaining anecdotes about anonymous clients who passed through his studio, as well as chapters about aerial and underground photography and the use of microphotography during the siege, the book is perversely devoid of information about the many years he spent photographing the cultural elite of his day.

How did Hugo behave when posing for a portrait? Sand? Dumas? Verne? Did the anarchist Bakunin make small talk? Félix never shares with us his impression of Sarah Bernhardt when she was barely out of her teens—or when she was a middle-aged diva known around the world as the Divine Sarah. A writer like Nadar with a flair for publicity and a sure grasp of a celebrity culture he helped to shape doesn't bury good material. And indeed, *Quand j'étais photographe* tells none of the stories one expects to hear because the author had other plans—big plans, naturally. Félix envisaged a vast autobiographical work that would complement the panorama of Parisian cultural life that he attempted with his portraits and his caricatures. At times he thought he would call this grand narrative *Mémoires des autres* (Memoirs of Others), at times *Faces et profils du XIXe siècle* (Faces and Profiles of the Nineteenth Century). Both titles reflect his instinct to tell his life story through the prism of his contemporaries—seventy-seven of them, to be exact. (How he came up with that number remains a mystery.) In many respects it was a promising project: though he hadn't kept a diary, he had stacks of letters from hundreds of correspondents, all carefully filed away; he also had plenty of experience as a curator of celebrities. But years of work on what came to be known as the *Cahiers Nadar* (Nadar Notebooks) never amounted to a finished manuscript.

He left a stack of false starts, outlines, rough drafts, and that curious document, *Charles Baudelaire intime,* published posthumously in 1911. If that's what *Mémoires des autres* was meant to look like, we would have been granted only fleeting glimpses of Nadar, bits of his story embedded in biographical investigations of his friends, with minimally edited chunks of correspondence wedged into the narrative. His autobiography would have been one long game of hide-and-seek with the reader. Félix concluded that explaining Baudelaire was a matter of "deciphering the indecipherable"; it may be that he planned to leave a similar legacy.

HIS LATER LIFE, like his later writing, was made up of fragments. He was no longer ruled by an all-consuming passion, as he was in his forties, when heavier-than-air was his principal preoccupation, or in his thirties, when it was the documenting, by caricature or photograph, the cultural elite of his day.

In the summer of 1873 Ernestine bought a house in the country that had belonged to her brother-in-law Adrien (who was obliged to sell to clear his debts). Tucked away on the edge of the Forest of Sénart, less than twenty miles south of Paris, *l'Ermitage* (the Hermitage) became the couple's refuge from the city, a bucolic retreat where Félix did his best to re-create the kind of close-knit community he'd known in his bohemian youth. Sénart was easy to reach by train, and a stream of Parisians came to visit the eccentric, vine-covered house almost swallowed by trees and surrounded by rambling walled orchard gardens and a gravel terrace. The building had been fashioned from the ruins of a convent. Upstairs were two vast studios, light pouring through high windows. On a cramped mezzanine, a warren of small rooms sufficed to house successive waves of visitors. On the ground floor was a big living room with a carved mantel over a generous fireplace; the walls were crowded with paintings and decorative porcelain plates. Cracks in the many mirrors were painted over with flowers. At once rustic and sophisticated, the house charmed even a skeptic like Edmond de Goncourt, who visited now and then in the company of Félix's near neighbors, the novelist Alphonse Daudet and his son Léon.

Another neighbor who sometimes dropped by to smoke a cigar with Félix on the terrace was Édouard Drumont, author in 1886 of

La France juive (Jewish France), a hugely successful two-volume anti-Semitic tract, and founder of the Ligue antisémitique de France (Anti-Semitic League of France). As founder and publisher of the mass circulation daily *La Libre parole*, Drumont led an anti-Semitic campaign directed against Jewish officers serving in the French Army. Through his newspaper, he became one of the most vocal accusers of Alfred Dreyfus, the artillery officer of Jewish descent falsely convicted of spying for the Germans. When Félix, who abhorred anti-Semitism but had no trouble tolerating Drumont, expressed his bitter disgust with *La France juive*, Drumont coolly remarked, *"Il est évident, mon cher Nadar, que nous nous entendrons toujours mais que nous nous entendrons rarement."* (It's evident, my dear Nadar, that we will always get along and rarely agree.)

Félix and Ernestine lived in Sénart on and off for nearly a quarter of a century, sometimes at ease, sometimes short of cash, always surrounded by friends, devoted servants, and a menagerie of animals that wandered in and out of the house. Among the many pets was Tocar (short for Photocar), a quarrelsome yellow mutt, scruffy and black-eyed, with whom Félix had a special bond.

He wrote his feuilletons. He composed endless letters, many of them as quarrelsome as Tocar, some full of cranky complaints. And he entertained: at long lunches full of talk, he held court, spinning tales, arguing, sermonizing, and dispensing anecdotes. He conjured up for his guests his personal pantheon, a snaking procession of men and women he'd known and admired.

He took up Sunday painting, happy to dab his brush and paint pretty pictures of his outdoor surroundings.

IMPOSSIBLE TO IMAGINE Félix in his youth taking up painting and not doing something unexpected with his new skill—creating the world's longest mural, say, or capturing cloudscapes from the basket of a balloon. But he never aspired to make a living with a paintbrush; it was an ordinary hobby, something he'd neither needed nor had time for until now. Félix had been domesticated.

In his thirties, influenced by Gautier and Baudelaire, he had become a prolific, somewhat scattershot art critic, producing for various magazines and newspapers what he called his *Nadar Jury*, written commentary (often incisive, occasionally wrongheaded) on the work displayed at official exhibitions; these were accompanied by his satirical caricatures of selected paintings. His deep respect for professional artists did nothing to temper his opinion of individual works, an opinion sometimes colored by what he knew of an artist's politics. Into his seventies he went on writing articles about art, among them a long, laudatory essay on Constantin Guys published in *Le Figaro* in 1892.

He also collected art, haphazardly. Already on the rue Saint-Lazare, the studio walls had been lined with canvases by Camille Corot, Doré, Daumier, Géricault, and Johan Jongkind. In 1859 he bought two landscapes for five thousand francs from his friend Charles-François Daubigny, whose portrait he exhibited that same year.

Like Corot, Daubigny was a Barbizon painter who influenced the Impressionists. He was famous for his floating studio, a refitted

ferry that opened up fresh river vistas and allowed him to study from midstream the effects of light on water. His fellow painter Zacharie Astruc described him as "tender, gentle, seductive," and "a man of delicious naivety, as unaffected as a child." Nadar used soft focus and wrapped him in an oversize wool coat, like a swaddling blanket, to convey precisely those qualities.

Zacharie Astruc was among the thirty artists represented in the inaugural exhibition of the Société anonyme coopérative des artistes peintres, sculpteurs, graveurs (Cooperative and Anonymous Association of Painters, Sculptors, and Engravers)—an event known today as the first Impressionist exhibition, featuring paintings by Cézanne, Degas, Monet, Morisot, Pissarro, Renoir, and Sisley. Because the show was held in Nadar's studio on the boulevard des Capucines (in April 1874, after he'd moved out, but while he still held the lease), it's often assumed that he was a supporter of the nascent Impressionist movement. Not exactly. He was happy to rent out the space to anyone willing to pay for it, even to Judith Gautier, the remarkable daughter of his friend Théophile, who used the space for Wagner concerts. Félix loathed Wagner, not least for the rabid joy the composer expressed when Prussia humiliated France on the battlefield.

The few remarks Félix made about Impressionism were mostly disparaging. He did, however, own paintings by one artist who was in the show, Eugène Boudin, and two others, Jongkind and Manet, who were invited to join the exhibition but declined. Manet was introduced to Félix by Baudelaire, who eventually made him see the importance of the painter's provocative and much-criticized work. To judge from the Nadar portrait, made in the early 1860s at the boulevard des Capucines studio, the force of the sitter's character made an immediate impact. The unsettling power of Manet's concentrated, almost angry gaze draws attention to the eyes, but it's perhaps the fist planted on the thigh that best conveys the sheer determination of a painter unfazed by scandal, unlikely ever to compromise his artistic principles.

Though Félix had no hand in the Impressionist show at 35, boulevard des Capucines, he did help arrange other exhibitions. The first, in 1878, was a retrospective of Daumier's work intended to raise money for the artist, who was living in a cottage in the countryside near Paris, blind and destitute. (He died the following year.) Nearly two decades later, Félix organized a posthumous exhibition of drawings and watercolors by Guys. The show, called *Visions de Constantin Guys, high life, low life,* opened in April 1895 at the fashionable Paris gallery of Georges Petit. Félix was always hoping to stoke a revival of interest in Guys, in part out of sincere admiration for the work, in part because Guys had given him over the years more than 450 drawings—and by 1895, the Nadar fortunes were at a low ebb.

<hr />

WHILE IT'S TRUE what Banville wrote ("I don't know any man less impressed with money than him"), it's also true that in his old age Félix was equally unimpressed by the absence of money—especially from his own pocket.

In the 1870s, after the disaster of *Le Géant* and the inevitable postsiege retrenchment, the name *Nadar,* renowned for so many reasons, became associated in certain circles with chronic financial distress. When in 1875 the waggish magazine editor and prolific author Pierre Véron published his satiric *Le Panthéon de poche* (Pocket Pantheon), he naturally devoted an entry to Félix, the man who'd made pantheons popular. It begins charmingly, with good-humored mockery and a handsome compliment, and concludes with a pointed allusion to Nadar's scramble for solvency:

> NADAR—Artist-*littérateur*-aeronaut-photographer of the wading bird variety.
>
> So tall, so tall, that it looks like he's carrying his own head on a pike.
>
> And what a strange gleaming head it is, looking like the sun is always setting behind it!
>
> A valiant nature, an instant wit like his collodion that assimilates at once everything that passes before his darkroom.
>
> If he'd wanted to, I bet he could have been a banker.
>
> He perhaps regrets not having wanted to.

The idea of Félix in charge of a bank is appalling, but so is the idea of Félix unable to live the large, careless life he'd always enjoyed, even as a penniless bohemian living on oysters in a dismal garret. Because he was so unfailingly generous to others, and others so generous with him; and because in his prime he was able to make and lose and make again astonishing amounts of money, he was ill prepared for the uncomfortable situation in which he found himself after turning over the studio to Paul. Once he'd officially retired, virtually his only income—the income he and Ernestine lived on—was a monthly dividend paid out of the revenue from the business. Over time that revenue diminished; by the early 1890s, the payments were coming late or not at all, which made life in Sénart uncomfortable and put considerable strain on relations between father and son.

There was a second, related problem: Paul was known as Paul Nadar, never as Paul Tournachon. In other words, Paul bore the name Félix had made for himself and fought for. Because father and son were both Nadar, the son's success (or lack thereof)—the success of the Nadar studio that Paul was now running—would inevitably have material bearing on the father's reputation, now and in the years to come. All this mattered to Félix; posterity mattered tremendously, it was fundamental to his career—to all his careers. A telling italicized phrase in the statement he filed with the court as part of his lawsuit against Adrien positively trembles with the intensity of his emotion: *"This name that belongs to me alone, this name, the principal patrimony I have to hand down to my child."* All in the same breath he reminds us of the huge importance he attached to his pseudonym, his intention to bequeath it to his son, and his reluctance to share it. It's a message mixed enough to induce whiplash: though he plans to hand it down, the name belongs to him alone.

If Paul thought he could solve the problem by signing photographs "P Nadar," he soon found out how wrong he was. Félix told him, "I admit to having trouble grasping the distinction you seem to be establishing between Nadar and Paul Nadar."

The weight of paternal expectation piled pressure on Paul, pressure intensified by perplexing paternal ambivalence. Following in the footsteps of the Great Nadar, bearing the same name, Paul had to run a business that would generate sufficient profit for himself and his parents, yet avoid in any way tarnishing or debasing the famous trademark above the entrance to the studio.

A third and final complication: passionate about the theater and especially about actresses, Paul in his mid-twenties became passionate about a particular actress at the Opéra-Comique, Marie Degrandi, who was married and the mother of a little girl. In 1883, a year after they met—but only after Degrandi had obtained a divorce—Paul told his mother that he was in love and wanted to marry, and asked for her maternal blessing. She refused. Having made inquiries, the otherwise mild, gentle, and forgiving Ernestine told her son that she could not consent to the marriage, that she never would. Unpleasant exchanges ensued, then an uneasy standoff that lasted a dozen years: Paul remained devoted to his mistress, Ernestine adamant that she would not give her blessing. Paul was free to marry, but his wife would not be welcome at the rue d'Anjou or at Sénart. Félix despised Degrandi, whose name he declined to utter, yet he remained above the fray—at least until Ernestine's health deteriorated, at which point he began to feel that Paul's behavior was a threat to his wife. He jumped in with his habitual vehemence, whereupon Ernestine felt obliged to mediate between father and son. With the unmentionable Degrandi offstage yet ever present, family life became a strained, unhappy affair.

IN THE FALL of 1886, Ernestine's doctor advised that she spend the winter in a warmer climate for the sake of her weak lungs. She and Félix traveled to Italy and stayed through the spring, spending time in Rome and Naples. They were in Florence in late May when they heard the news that a terrible fire had gutted the Opéra-Comique, with hundreds feared dead. (The actual death toll was eighty-four.) Ernestine was convinced her son was among the casualties. He wasn't—but the shock was too much for her: the stroke she suffered the next morning paralyzed her left side. She never regained full use of her left arm or leg.

Partial paralysis was only the most recent addition to Ernestine's burden. Being married to Félix was a hazard even when there were no balloons in sight. Along with the obsessions, extravagance, and nonstop commotion, she may also have had to put up with an infidelity or two, traces of which are evident in the groveling letters he sent pledging devotion to her alone. Her habitual posture was mute forgiveness, his to beat his chest and loudly proclaim his remorse, his worthlessness, and his wife's unparalleled virtue.

He'd always been caring and attentive with his Madame Bonne (especially, perhaps, when his affections were engaged elsewhere). Now that she was partly incapacitated, he ministered to her with remarkable tenderness. Edmond de Goncourt, always ambivalent about Félix, paid a visit to Sénart in the summer of 1893 and recorded his impressions in the journal he'd begun four decades earlier with his late brother Jules: in the middle of a motley crowd of guests gathered in the garden was the reclining figure of Ernestine, wrapped in a sky-blue dressing gown with pink silk lining. Nadar hovered around her, rearranging her bright robe, brushing back the hair on her temples, showering her with caresses. On another occasion, Goncourt was leaving Sénart with the Daudets who, as they climbed into their carriage, invited Félix to bring Ernestine to their house for dinner. Goncourt noticed that their kind gesture brought tears to Félix's eyes.

THE THREE SIMMERING family conflicts boiled over during the first half of 1894. The studio finances suffered a further collapse; Paul, age thirty-eight, demanded that he be allowed to marry *with his parents' blessing;* and he then insisted that his father sign over to him exclusive ownership of the name *Nadar.*

Paroxysms of outrage from Félix. Operatic letters full of angry oaths and imprecations flew back and forth between father and son. Félix felt his very identity was being threatened—his self was being usurped. In one of his notebooks he wrote, "He jealously, greedily, hatefully wishes that I had not existed before him and that he had been me." It was Paul he was writing about, but it might as well have been Adrien four decades earlier—the difference being that back then Félix had been fighting for a principle and for the sake of a studio in which he would create photographic masterpieces. Now he was merely embroiled in a family dispute over money and marriage and dealing with the natural consequence of having thoroughly overshadowed his son.

After a long and fraught arbitration, with three friends acting as mediators, Félix relinquished his share of the business—but *not* the right to the pseudonym. Paul Nadar and Marie Degrandi were married in July 1894 (and divorced twenty years later).

There's a pattern to Félix's family quarrels: intense drama and bitter feelings but an underlying devotion to duty, whether it be filial, fraternal, or paternal. Proudly unconventional in most respects, he took a rigidly conventional view of family obligations. The filial bond was to him a matter of "sacred duty," yet he and his mother fought so fiercely that she moved out of their shared apartment, taking her furniture with her. Reconciliation followed almost immediately. As for his brother, when Félix wasn't suing Adrien, he was going out of his way to encourage and support him—and continued to do so until Adrien's death early in 1903. The quarrel with Paul would follow the same pattern: Adrien's final illness, an aggressive onslaught of dementia, brought father and son back together again.

But for the moment, during the crisis of 1894, bad blood ruled. Writing to an old friend, Félix referred to his only child as "our most bitter enemy, the most venomous, our executioner."

⚬

FAR FROM KILLING HIM, his son's behavior gave him a new lease on life. In 1895, age seventy-five, now certain that Paul wouldn't be taking care of his two elderly parents, Félix went back to work. He traveled to Marseilles to look for fresh opportunities, came home dejected, persevered, found a property opposite Marseilles's Grand Hotel, and established a new studio, his fourth—a miniature, sun-drenched version of 35, boulevard des Capucines.

His principal contribution to the new business was his name: as at the rue d'Anjou, his work with the camera was limited. When a celebrity showed up to have his or her portrait taken—which they did in sufficient numbers to make the venture fashionable, then profitable—he would appear and dispense charm to his customers and advice to his assistants. The studio became a rendezvous for writers and journalists eager to hear stories about Nadar's Paris.

In 1899 he ceded his interest in the business to two women, close family friends who had helped care for Ernestine. They in turn promised to pay Félix an annuity of six thousand francs.

He remained in Marseilles until early 1904—"bubbling, astonishing, dazzling and lovable Marseilles," he called it. But as Banville said, he was Parisian to the tip of his fingernails, and after seven years it was time to go home, where he and his wife would be near their son, now no longer estranged.

Just before leaving Marseilles for good, Félix produced this re-markable document:

> *I, the undersigned, give to my son Paul Tournachon*
> *authorization to take for his name, personally or for business*
> *purposes, my pseudonym Nadar which remains excellently*
> *mine.*
>
>

G. *Félix Tournachon*

Nadar

Marseilles 17 December 1903
>

Hard to say whether this settled the question or made it more perplexing.

BACK IN PARIS, the couple lived modestly in a small apartment at 49, avenue d'Antin (now the avenue Franklin-D.-Roosevelt), not far from the place de l'Étoile. Gregarious as ever, even as the cohort of friends his own age dwindled rapidly, he indulged in nostalgia for the benefit of a press corps eager for anecdotes about the golden age of bohemia. Though he liked to reminisce, he remained essen-tially forward-looking. Aviation, still in its infancy, thrilled him, and he developed a fascination with international trade unions, which he believed would usher in an era of world peace. He stopped taking photographs.

In the last known photograph of him, he's sitting in a garden with his newspaper and pipe, a dapper old gentleman in good shoes,

black cravat, and the same combination of waistcoat and long jacket he'd been wearing his entire adult life.

He looks content and calm—perhaps he was—and remarkably like the young bohemian who sketched a self-portrait with pipe some fifty years earlier.

TWO DECADES AFTER the stroke that left her partially paralyzed, Ernestine died at home on January 3, 1909, age seventy-two.

Is there a better way to say good-bye to this long-suffering, endlessly forgiving woman, a wife who earned twice over the nickname Madame Bonne, than to look again at the photograph her husband took of her in about 1890, the image that prompted Roland Barthes to declare Nadar the world's greatest photographer?

Barthes posited a link between photography, madness, and pity. A few minutes communing with this image is all it takes to see that he may have been right. Madness and pity are mixed up in the urge to read her thoughts and feelings; in the hopeful illusion that we can know what she knew and feel what she felt, that the photo really does show us an "intimate resemblance," as Félix would say; and in the hard, hopeless truth that her inner life remains a mystery, that she is a stranger to us as we all are to each other, even husband and wife, parent and child.

That hard truth shouldn't stop us from wondering what Ernestine saw when she sat posing for Nadar with a sprig of violets pressed to her lips. I like to think that she saw a man she loved, a maddening, enchanting man doing the one thing he did better than anyone else, letting his strange genius flourish one last time.

BORN BEFORE THE invention of photography, Félix died on March 21, 1910, a few weeks shy of his ninetieth birthday, eight months after a French aviator, Louis Blériot, crossed the English Channel in a monoplane, vindicating Félix's belief that someday man would take off "prompt like electricity," soar, and touch down "like a bird at the desired spot." He sent a telegram congratulating the pilot and expressing the gratitude and joy of an "antediluvian" campaigner for heavier-than-air flight. Reprinted in *La Presse,* the telegram was Nadar's last public act, his final farewell.

XII

APRÈS NADAR

HUNDREDS OF NADAR OBITUARIES FROM ALL OVER France were published in the last week of March 1910. The note repeatedly struck was his connection with great figures of the previous century, Balzac, Baudelaire, Nerval, Hugo, Sand. His friendship with Murger and the bohemians of the 1840s featured prominently: poverty and solidarity endured and enjoyed a lifetime ago. The variety of his many careers—writer, caricaturist, photographer, balloonist—was another keynote. His radical politics were almost always mentioned, often with reference to a red jacket or a red beret, along with his boundless capacity for hope. There were many tributes to his energy and daring, his warm heart and legendary charm. Although he was referred to as an artist, there was usually no specific mention of photography as the locus of his genius.

Across the Atlantic, the *New York Times* caught the drift with its obituary, published on March 27. The headline emphasizes a very public gregariousness: FAMED BOULEVARDIER DEAD. The subhead cites what the paper presumably saw as his most significant accomplishment: "Félix Nadar Was Regarded as Father of Aeroplane Idea." According to the article itself, he was "one of those peculiar characters that could be produced nowhere but in France." Listing his occupations as "journalist, caricaturist, dilettante, Communard, aeronaut, and photographer," the *Times* asserted that "in each of these capacities he became famous." The red hair gets a mention, as does his personal association with "hundreds" of the "noted men" of his time. A month and a half later, the *Times* again lamented the disappearance of Nadar, "one of the most seductive and picturesque of typically Parisian personalities."

It was a *personality* that these eulogists chose to celebrate, a larger-than-life character, the last survivor of a generation of giants. This refrain predated his demise. His friend the novelist Anatole France, writing at the end of 1903 in Nadar's last autograph album, set the tone with praise so fulsome, one suspects a dash of irony: "Nadar is the best of men, the most inventive and the most courageous, the most tender, the proudest and the most charming. If we had kept the power to create mythical characters, Nadar would be in France what Daedalus was among the ancient Greeks." Presumably he meant Daedalus the artist and craftsman as well as airborne Daedalus.

There's a kind of poetic justice at work here. In all his professions, Nadar relied on the cult of celebrity to sell his work, whether it was a feuilleton, a caricature, or a photograph. Now his tireless efforts as a publicist returned to haunt his posthumous reputation: he was mourned not as an artist with a particular genius but as a boulevardier, a celebrity who consorted with celebrities. The reputation of this man who'd poked his nose into everything was now parceled out among various interested parties: to balloon enthusiasts, he was a pioneer aeronaut; to science fiction fans, he was the model for Verne's Michel Ardan; to fans of cartooning, he was the creator of *Mossieu Réac* and thus one of the godfathers of the comic strip.

The *Panthéon-Nadar* was already recognized as a national treasure during Félix's lifetime: three years before his death, the Bibliothèque Nationale de France bought the 587 portraits he made while assembling his epic lithograph, which remains an essential artifact of nineteenth-century French culture.

To students of the history of photography, Nadar was always a paragon, his fame in this respect boosted by an exhibition at the Bibliothèque Nationale in 1965. The catalog acknowledged the breadth and variety of his achievements and rightly pointed out that "a Nadar retrospective is of an era as well as of a man." But the photographs stole the show: the Nadar on display was an "incomparable" portraitist.

Three Nadar biographies have been published in French. (None of them has been translated.) The first, a slim, well-documented volume with a no-nonsense, just-the-facts attitude, appeared in 1966. The second, published fifteen years later, was freewheeling and made the case for a heroic Nadar whose accomplishments, despite his fame, were undervalued; its author was particularly keen to promote Nadar the writer. The third, published in 2010, established a new benchmark for Gallic arrogance with its very first sentence: *"Qui ne connaît Nadar?"* (Who doesn't know Nadar?)

It's true that by this time he'd earned a secure position in the history of art. A massive exhibition of his photography in the summer of 1994 at the Musée d'Orsay in Paris (which traveled the following year to the Metropolitan Museum of Art in New York) established beyond doubt that Nadar was one of the great portrait photographers of all time. (Five years later curators at the J. Paul Getty Museum in Los Angeles had the cute idea of organizing a show called *Nadar/Warhol: Paris/New York*. To be linked with Andy Warhol as a self-publicizing connoisseur of celebrity! Here was proof that Félix had achieved superstar status.)

I saw the exhibition at the Metropolitan Museum, and Nadar instantly claimed a place in my private pantheon of great artists. But as John Updike observed in his review of the show, "Photography is a matter of time"—nearly twenty years passed before I tried to find out about Nadar's life. The catalyst was Julian Barnes's *Levels of Life*, an unusual book, part essay, part short story, part memoir, in which Barnes briefly sketches the contours of Nadar's curious career and irrepressible character. Thanks to Barnes, Félix charmed me, as he had charmed so many others. And so I went back to the photographs to look again.

APPENDIX

MEMENTOS OF NADAR'S WORLD

THE BOOK, THE SIZE OF A LARGE PHOTO ALBUM, HAS BEEN disassembled, its two hundred–odd pages cut out and placed each in its own transparent protective sheath. Detached, the leather-bound front cover, with Nadar's flamboyant signature stamped in the center in gold leaf, lies in a cardboard box looking scuffed and forlorn, like exiled royalty.

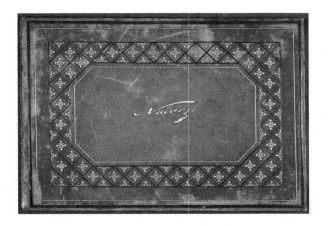

The album is a *livre d'or*, one of several guest books or auto-graph albums he kept in successive studios. If you came to sit for a portrait (or a caricature, in the early days on the rue Saint-Lazare), and if you were an artist or a celebrity or preferably both, he would pester you to sign and leave a memento: a quip, a sketch, a poem, a few bars of music. Most sitters complied. Many signed and left only a brief remark, if any; others spent hours over a drawing or a

watercolor, leaving on the page work of impressive quality. Félix
was very proud of his collection of autographs, each one a token of
friendship or a link with an eminent individual.

This particular *livre d'or*, an astonishing record of the rich cultural life of Paris during the Second Empire, is stored in a rare
book library in Philadelphia, Pennsylvania. Philadelphia? Suffering from one of his periodic bouts of acute insolvency, Félix sold
the album at auction in the early 1890s. It was bought by Thomas
W. Evans, an American expatriate living in Paris who'd grown
rich and respected as the dentist to Napoléon III. When Evans died
in 1897, he left his considerable fortune to endow the Thomas W.
Evans Museum and Dental Institute; the *livre d'or* and his collection
of art and antiques were shipped across the Atlantic and housed
in the Evans Building, an imposing Tudor Revival edifice erected
on the site of his ancestral home, in what is now the middle of the
University of Pennsylvania campus. After languishing for decades
in the Dental Medicine Library, the Nadar album was transferred
in 1985 to the university's rare books and manuscripts collection.
About ten years ago it was taken apart and filed away in fourteen
cardboard storage boxes.

Few people know it exists; fewer ask to see it. Yet even dis-
bound it evokes the busy ferment of Nadar's world in the decade
after Louis-Napoléon's coup d'état—the decade in which Félix
attempted to create a panorama of his illustrious contemporaries.
The pages of the *livre d'or* echo with the voices of talented men
(only a handful of women signed the album, mostly opera singers,
actresses, and ballerinas), and these voices make many different
sounds: friendly greeting; mutual admiration; facetious commentary; and political harangue (mostly socialist). Self-conscious musings and private jokes abound, and always in the background is
the buzz of artistic ego, sometimes muted, sometimes not. It's clear
that an element of competition was involved: anybody about to
sign would flip through to see what had been done before and by
whom. Then there was the delicate business of choosing a page.
With whom would you like to be associated?

Nadar's photographs show us what the cultural elite of his day
looked like, the images preserved by the modern miracle of the

wet-plate collodion process. A *livre d'or* makes use of an older, more primitive method to offer a different perspective: the traces it preserves are marks on plain paper left by the individual's own hand.

On the first page, a pair of writers pop up, Léon Gozlan and Fabrice Labrousse. Each left a sentence and a signature, one on top of the other, like lines of dialogue. The two men were almost exact contemporaries, and both wrote for the theater; they must have known each other but probably visited Nadar's studio on different days—a pause in the dialogue. A close associate of Balzac, and like Balzac wildly prolific, Gozlan scrawled in his neat but impulsive hand a pronouncement Félix would have endorsed enthusiastically: "Nothing is more immoral than boredom." Labrousse's rejoinder—"Nothing is more moral than distraction"—would also have appealed. The rest of the page is blank, as though there were nothing more to say.

This *livre d'or* is a treasure house of distraction. To give a sense of what it would be like to page through it knowing something of the story behind each signature and each memento, I've picked out and commented on about a quarter of the four hundred illustrious contemporaries who grace its pages.

THÉOPHILE GAUTIER, WHOSE first ambition was to be a painter, sketched a girl's head, a pretty ink drawing, delicate, unfussy. The garland in the girl's hair is suggested with a light, decorative touch. Dreamy and romantic, she reminds us that Félix's friend Le Théos, in addition to his Olympian self-confidence, had a tender side.

GAUTIER'S ITALIAN WIFE, Ernesta Grisi, signed the album along with her sister Carlotta, the prima ballerina who was the first to dance in the title role of *Giselle,* for which Gautier wrote the scenario. The Grisi sisters left no comment, but next to their signatures is a short, sharp quip scrawled by the ardent feminist and world traveler Olympe Audouard: "Man is selfishness personified."

GÉRARD DE NERVAL wrote out two poems, almost certainly on separate visits. The first, a celebrated lyric, "Vers Dorés" (Golden Sayings), warns against mankind's hubris and insists on the spirit lurking in all matter ("everything is sentient"). It's written in a flowing, assertive hand and signed with a bold flourish; no date is indicated. Below is an enigmatic quatrain originally composed, according to Nerval, on the back of a receipt from the press magnate Polydore Millaud, Félix's benefactor. The rhymes play on the value of money and the value of a poet's signature—his autograph; Nerval was dead broke at the time, and Félix had most likely arranged a loan from Millaud. The quatrain is squeezed under "Vers Dorés" in cramped handwriting; it's dated November 1, 1854, less than three months before Nerval hanged himself.

The shock of that suicide echoes jarringly in the sardonic comments dashed off on the same page (to the right of "Vers Dorés") by Auguste Villemot, a columnist for *Le Figaro* who fancied himself a wit and often signed his columns "Bourgeois de Paris":

> It is better to be seated than standing;
> It is better to be lying down than seated;
> It is better to be dead than lying down.

Villemot credits the saying to the medieval Persian poet Saadi (a dubious attribution) and appends a question: "Could this maxim be an advertisement for an undertaker?" It's possible that Félix was amused by Villemot's wisecrack (this was a milieu obsessed with the uses and abuses of publicity), but I doubt it. When Félix wrote about his "gentle" friend Gérard, both before and after his death, there was never any hint of irreverence.

———————

POLYDORE MILLAUD LEFT two words only: *Être utile* (To be useful), surely his motto vis-à-vis Félix and his impecunious bohemian friends.

———————

UNDER A FEW BARS of music from *Il trovatore* and Giuseppe Verdi's flamboyant signature, Auguste Lireux, undoubtedly aware that Verdi had composed seventeen operas in the last twelve years, wrote "Laziness is man's finest attribute." To which Pierre Joigneaux, a radical socialist and passionate agronomist with a special interest in viticulture, responded with lighthearted disapproval: "In my capacity as a farmer, I protest."

Lireux, a pugnacious journalist who wrote principally about politics and theater, was from 1842 to 1845 the director of the Théâtre de l'Odéon. In 1848, when Hetzel and Félix founded *La Revue comique,* they chose Lireux as editor in chief. Four years later, when the empire was declared, he reaped the reward for his many attacks on Louis-Napoléon: he was arrested and sentenced to be deported to a penal colony. That sentence was commuted to exile, but the banishment lasted only a few months.

A SELF-CONSCIOUSLY contrarian crew resisted the call to leave more than the bare minimum. Most were being funny, some were being grumpy (possibly irritated by Félix's insistence). It's unlikely that anyone was being shy.

The science writer and militant socialist Victor Meunier wrote, "Here is a line of my handwriting." On the opposite end of the political spectrum, Louis Veuillot, who dedicated his career to the cause of papal supremacy, left an equally dry message: "Here is my handwriting for Mr. Nadar." (The word *Nadar* is scribbled over, as if it had been misspelled and corrected.)

Louis de Cormenin, a writer and a jurist, left only a bland greeting: "*Bonjour* Nadar."

Félix's favorite musician, the actor, singer, and composer Joseph Darcier, wrote only *Par obéissance* (Out of obedience) and scratched a hasty signature. According to Félix, Darcier's talent lay in making popular music, "the art of the people, true art, the only art possible today."

Auguste Maquet, who was introduced to Alexandre Dumas by Nerval and went on to collaborate with him on *The Three Musketeers*, *The Count of Monte-Cristo*, and sixteen other novels, scratched out the phrase "Good for one autograph"—and signed his name.

"To make people pose and then to make them write, that's making them pose too much, my friend Nadar." That was the cynical observation of the magnificently named Charles de Matharel de Fiennes, a journalist who sometimes signed his work with the pseudonym *Senneif*—his last name backward.

"I'm not signing this year," wrote Gustave Louis Chaix d'Est-Ange, and signed—a paradox worthy of Magritte. Chaix d'Est-Ange was an eminent lawyer whose son, Gustave Gaspard Chaix d'Est-Ange, also a lawyer, was unsuccessful in defending Baudelaire in court against the charge that *Les Fleurs du mal* was an "outrage against public morals."

The famous actor Prosper Bressant, who spent eight years in Russia at the French theater in St. Petersburg before his debut at the

Comédie-Française in 1846, made use of a dramatic pause: "What could I possibly write? Oh, I know! The devil take albums!"

Should Étienne Arago be numbered among the cranky and the reluctant? He left a hurried ink drawing, possibly a self-portrait, of a bearded man in a striped jacket smoking a pipe. Next to it he wrote: "I know of nothing more respectable than blank paper."

The youngest of six brothers, Arago had a remarkable, tumultuous career in theater, journalism, and politics. He co-wrote a novel with Balzac; co-founded *Le Figaro;* directed the Théâtre du Vaudeville, which burned down, bankrupting him; fought on the barricades in 1830 and 1848; and served briefly, after the fall of Napoléon III, as mayor of Paris. But he wasn't the most famous of his siblings (that was François Arago, a brilliant physicist and statesman); nor was his career the most spectacular. (That would be Jacques Arago, who in 1817 sailed around the world on a scientific expedition that lasted three years, went blind in 1837, and in 1853 wrote a book-length account of his circumnavigation— *without ever using the letter "a"*—and died two years later, in Rio de Janeiro.) And yet Étienne Arago's name will most certainly live on, if only because of his contribution to philately: as head of the post office in 1848, he was responsible for issuing the first French postal stamp.

And then there's Constantin Guys, self-taught master of the watercolor sketch, the man Baudelaire championed as "the painter of modern life." Guys left no drawing, not even a doodle, which must have disappointed Félix but probably didn't surprise him: at once difficult and publicity-shy, Guys rarely signed his work—you could ask for a drawing or an autograph but not both. At the top edge of a page he wrote: "A pen, a paintbrush: what to do, and why bother?"—and signed that characteristically curt comment with a flourish.

Just below Guys's signature is a watercolor, by Pierre-Luc-Charles Cicéri, of a boulder and a spindly bush, pretty enough but indistinct. Cicéri's passion (and his profession) was painting sets for the opera. Was Guys's gruff shrug a comment on Cicéri's contribution (and his profession)?

Guys ran away from home at eighteen to join Byron's expedition and fight for Greek independence; he later joined a French dragoon regiment. Switching from soldier to tutor, he taught French and drawing to the grandchildren of a celebrated English watercolorist, Thomas Girtin. In the late 1840s Guys was hired as an illustrator—in effect, a reporter who drew instead of wrote—by the *Illustrated London News*. In 1848 the paper sent him to Paris to cover the February Revolution. His dispatches during the mid-1850s were from the Crimean War battlefields; he compiled a visual record of that conflict that Baudelaire considered superior to any account, written or otherwise.

Living in Paris in the 1860s, Guys trained his eagle eye on the everyday activity of the capital, producing watercolors Félix praised as fresh and full of life, with none of the stale odor of the museum. Though they do have a spontaneous feel, Guys's sketches were invariably executed from memory: he would look, then go home and draw. Among his favorite subjects were women and girls of all social classes. He reveled in Second Empire fashions. And he never tired of sketching horses and horse-drawn carriages. Which brings us to the cruel ending of his career: on July 21, 1885, at the age of eighty-two, after a dinner at Félix's house, Guys was run over by a carriage on the rue du Havre, and one leg was crushed. He spent the last seven years of his long life in bedridden penury, refusing offers of hospitality from Félix and others.

When he looked back on his friendship with Guys, Félix felt obliged to separate the artist, whom he thought very great, from the man, whose rigid military manners he often found intolerable. "I still haven't forgiven him," Félix wrote, "his ingratitude toward Baudelaire, to whom he owed so much."

BAUDELAIRE'S OWN CONTRIBUTION to the *livre d'or* was to write out the eight stanzas of "Le Reniement de Saint Pierre" (The Denial of Saint Peter) from *Les Fleurs du mal*. The famous dandy had a dandy's mannered handwriting, surprisingly legible and incongruously decorated with curlicues—filigree for a poem that is a shockingly bitter meditation on human suffering and divine indifference.

PERHAPS THE ODDEST page of the album consists of fantastical doodles of grotesque goblins and monsters by Baudelaire's friend Armand du Mesnil, a bureaucrat who worked doggedly in the ministry of education for forty years, a career he embarked on after his father decamped for America and left him to care for his mother and a young niece. Though his day job was a necessity, he yearned for the literary life; according to his old pal Théodore de Banville, du Mesnil had a "lyrical soul always overflowing with poetry and dreams." In his free time, he wrote plays and stories. Later, too busy to write but still loyal to the bohemian ideals of his youth, he used his government position to advance a series of petitions on behalf of Baudelaire. It was hoped that a state pension might help relieve the poet's chronic debt. Du Mesnil's efforts met with partial success: from time to time Baudelaire received from the ministry grants of several hundred francs. But no pension was forthcoming, not even when he was paralyzed by a stroke in 1866 and a succession of prominent literary figures added their voices to the latest petition.

The curious du Mesnil doodles include a rabbit-like creature with alarming teeth and claws; running human legs that meet at a crotch that is a face; a knock-kneed humanoid with the head of a cross-eyed bird; and a skinny goblin skipping rope. The gothic flavor of the drawings is a reminder that tales of supernatural horror were enormously popular at the time. Baudelaire, the keen-eyed apostle of modernity, was as famous for having translated Poe as he was for the scandal of *Les Fleurs du mal*. The daydreams of his friend du Mesnil, the kind-hearted government bureaucrat whose career obliged him to be the servant of the orderly and the rational, were populated with nightmare monsters, surreal creatures crawling out of the unconscious.

Reminiscing at the end of his life about Baudelaire and their bohemian heyday, Félix enumerated the friends he would meet in the poet's company, among them "the excellent Armand du Mesnil."

AN EXTENDED COMIC RIFF on vaudeville and artistic collaboration begins at the top of one page with an aphorism left by Marc-Antoine-Amédée Michel (who wrote as Marc-Michel). "Distraction is the daughter of wit," he announced, echoing the album's earliest entries "and the mother of silliness." Below, as if to prove his point, two of his collaborators, Eugène Labiche and Auguste Lefranc (the same Lefranc who took credit for bestowing Félix's pseudonym by transforming *Tournachon* into *Tournadard*), mixed wit and silliness in rhymed verses. Marc-Michel, Labiche, and Lefranc all wrote for the vaudeville stage, at one point adopting a collective pseudonym, *Paul Dandré*. Their humor is mostly frothy, good-natured nonsense. And yet Labiche, whose father was a prosperous Parisian grocer, was a tremendously talented comic writer. Late in life he was accorded the highest honor of the literary establishment, election to the Académie Française; his farces are still performed today in French theaters. As for Lefranc, he started out as a lawyer, succumbed to the lure of bohemia, eased into theatrical circles thanks in part to a family connection (he was a cousin of Eugène Scribe, arguably the most successful French playwright of the nineteenth century), wrote scores of vaudeville comedies, and in middle age quit the theater to become a banker. Lefranc was one of the investors in the studio at 35, boulevard des Capucines—and one of Félix's more exigent creditors.

EUGÈNE SCRIBE ACHIEVED what most of the writers Félix knew only dreamed about: he was elected to the Académie Française in 1834, at age forty-two—and made himself fabulously rich and world famous through writing. When he died in 1861, the obituary in the *New York Times* declared him "the most prolific, versatile and popular playwright of France."

Scribe's success was due at least in part to his production line methods: he employed a team of collaborators (and shared credit where due). His workshop churned out plays, operas, and novels at a dizzy clip. His writings for theater alone fill twenty volumes.

In the *livre d'or*, Scribe copied down the inscription carved over the door of Séricourt, the splendid château he bought in 1835: *Le théâtre a payé cet asile champêtre! Vous qui passez, merci? . . . Je vous le dois peut-être!!* (The theater paid for this pastoral haven! You who are passing by, thank you? . . . Perhaps it's to you that I owe it!!)

THE ANARCHIST Pierre-Joseph Proudhon, author of the slogan "Property is theft," thundered, "After the persecutors, I know nothing more detestable than the martyrs."

Many pages later, another anarchist pops up: the Russian aristocrat turned tireless revolutionary Mikhail Alexandrovich Bakunin, who signed his name in the French manner, Bakounine. Visiting on August 7, 1862, he left this enigmatic warning: "Watch out that liberty doesn't come to you from the north." Just a year earlier he'd made a daring escape from perpetual exile in Siberia.

Below Bakunin's signature is an ink wash sketch by Jean-François Millet of a pair of clogs, as plain and honest as a big toe. Félix considered Millet one of the best living French painters; he praised his art as "essentially democratic."

Bakunin and Millet—what a confluence! Did Bakunin spot the clogs and feel that this realist depiction was a good match for his political convictions? Or did Millet see Bakunin's signature and feel moved to leave an emblem of humble peasantry? Or was it just serendipity?

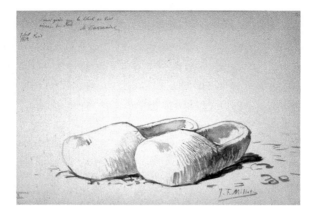

FÉLIX'S OLDEST FRIEND, Charles Asselineau, jotted down an endearingly goofy poem about the muse in a quandary, unable to decide whether she favors Tournachon or Nadar (Nadar has more art, Tournachon is more nicely turned out)—a reminder that Asselineau knew Félix Tournachon well before Nadar came into being. The more one learns about the gentle, modest Asselineau, who lived for books and wrote sane, measured criticism of both literature and art, the more he seems the perfect match and foil for Félix—the one grounded and circumspect, the other bold and impetuous, both brilliant in their way, both blessed with a talent for friendship.

On the same page with Asselineau is Alexandre Dumas *père*. It could be that Dumas's wry contribution was provoked by the silly doggerel left by Asselineau and others. In messy handwriting, he proposed "a rule of proportion" clearly learned from backstage collaborations at the theater: if the show was cobbled together in seventy-six hours, how long did it take to write the song?

On another page, presumably after another visit, the great man left a capably executed pencil drawing of the head and shoulders of a young woman in a bonnet and shawl.

Nadar's early portrait of Dumas, possibly taken the same day the drawing was made, shows us an author brimming with self-confidence, hands piled jauntily on top of his

cane as though he were suppressing with ease all doubt, all anxiety, all disturbance. He seems also to be suppressing a smile, maintaining the dignity of the pose despite the barrage of Félix's banter.

CHARLES JEAN-BAPTISTE JACQUOT, who wrote under the name Eugène de Mirecourt, had the same impulse as Félix—both wanted to present to posterity a panorama of their illustrious contemporaries—but Félix achieved his aim with talent and charm. Blessed with neither of those qualities, Mirecourt relied on dogged persistence (he eventually published 140 biographical essays), a strong moralizing streak (sadly undermined by the hypocrisy of his brazen willingness to peddle malicious gossip, rumor, and misinformation), and an absolute conviction that the private lives of "great men" should be made public.

One of Mirecourt's scoops was that Dumas, like Scribe, produced his hugely successful work in collaboration with other writers. In 1845 Mirecourt published a vicious pamphlet called *Fabrique de Romans: Maison Alexandre Dumas et Cie* (The Novel

Factory: The Firm of Alexandre Dumas & Co). Balzac read it and remarked, "It's unspeakably stupid, but sadly true. . . . And since in France more credence is given to witty calumny than to truth stupidly articulated, it will do little harm to Dumas." In fact, Mirecourt's litany of insults—the ugliest of which played on the fact that Dumas's father's mother was a black woman, an African-born slave on a plantation in the Caribbean—did him no harm at all.

Dumas sued for libel and won: Mirecourt was sentenced to fifteen days in prison. Badly battered at the time, Mirecourt's literary reputation has since shrunk to nothing.

The trace he left in Nadar's album is an eighteen-line poem full of arch classical allusion with an earthy twist at the end: "Come then, kiss me, my dear/ A good lover is worth all the gods." He has the entire page to himself—no one was inclined to share it.

GUSTAVE DORÉ'S CHARCOAL sketch of a furious folkdance in the courtyard of a country inn is a whirlwind, bravura performance. How long would it have taken him to capture the energy of the six dancers, the grotesque musicians, the dopey onlookers, the frantic dog, the outraged geese? Fifteen minutes? A half-hour?

When he was finished, he scrawled a dedication to his "good friend" Nadar. The drawing is undated, but I like to think that it was made in 1854, the year Doré was busy illustrating an edition of Rabelais's rude, earthy comedy, *The Life of Gargantua and of Pantagruel.*

————— ❖ —————

ONE PAGE IS crowded with grandees of various stripes: the composer Gioachino Rossini, the poet Alfred de Musset, the religious thinker Félicité de Lamennais, and the historian Jules Michelet. Clearly drawn to the luster of those great names are four others: the comte de Soyecourt, an otherwise obscure scion of an ancient noble family; Antoine Petroz, a quack pharmacist who is counted among the pioneers of homeopathy; Louis Boyer, a minor playwright; and a critic, Charles Blanc, the younger brother of the socialist philosopher and politician Louis Blanc, one of Félix's heroes.

A notorious gourmand who had stopped composing operas twenty-five years earlier, Rossini left a sloppy signature over equally sloppy musical notation. As a caption for the *Lanterne magique* caricature of the composer of *The Barber of Seville*, Félix wrote: "What do you want me to tell you about this one? He's the master,—he's Rossini. That's all there is to it!"

Musset wrote out a stanza about a blissful fat pheasant scratching its tummy in the sun, a fragment from his long narrative poem *Namouna.* He also drew the bare outline of a little church, with the moon over the steeple like the dot on an *i.* A prodigy, a dandy, and famously the lover of George Sand (it ended badly), Musset died young, his weak heart damaged by drink.

Lamennais had been one of Félix's father's prized authors. But instead of quoting from *Essay on Indifference in Matters of Religion,* the early book that Victor published so successfully, the firebrand theologian wrote out in a precise hand, "Young soldier, where are you going?"—a refrain from *Words of a Believer,* his hugely influential best seller. Could this be an allusion to Félix's ill-fated mission to liberate Poland by force, on foot? Lamennais had been an early and powerful voice calling for French intervention on behalf of the oppressed Polish people, and the police file on Félix specified that he was "one of the most enterprising of Mr. Lamennais's hench-man." Though "henchman" is surely a paranoid exaggeration, it would be nice to think Lamennais knew of and approved Félix's quixotic gesture.

"Young soldier, where are you going?"—just below that melancholy phrase, the brilliant Michelet left a tribute to his old pal Lamennais: "In this house of magic . . . I'm happy to greet my master and I've written my name at his feet."

———◦✦◦———

THE GONCOURT BROTHERS, inescapably themselves, boasted of their jaundiced detachment: "Skepticism is a good stall from which to view life."

———◦✦◦———

SKETCHES OF FÉLIX were left by Alexandre Laemlein, Jean Gigoux, Prince Alexis Soltykoff, Alcide Joseph Lorentz, and Charles Amédée de Noé (better known as the cartoonist Cham).

A Bavarian-born history painter, Laemlein was admitted to the École des Beaux-Arts at age sixteen to study with a neoclassical painter, Jean-Baptiste Regnault, who promptly died, and then another, François-Édouard Picot—the same Picot who taught Félix's brother, Adrien.

In his review of the Salon of 1846, Baudelaire paused to mention a painting by Laemlein, *Universal Charity*:

> [A] charming woman holds by the hand and carries at her breast kids from every climate, white, yellow black, etc. . . . Certainly Mr. Laemlein has an eye for color; but there's a major flaw in this painting, which is that the little Chinese boy is so pretty, and his robe makes such an agreeable effect that it almost monopolizes the eye of the spectator. The little mandarin is still trotting along in one's memory.

Somber, handsome, ambitious, Laemlein's monochrome ink and watercolor portrait of Félix strains with some success for the psychological acuity of a Nadar photograph.

Gigoux tries less hard and does better. His rapid sketch, focused on the eyes, gives the impression of vitality—the quality so many of his friends remarked on. Félix looks as though he's just noticed something interesting and is about to jump up and investigate.

A talented and versatile painter, Gigoux is today remembered for having been the lover of Balzac's widow, the Polish noblewoman Ewelina Hańska. In 1851, a year after Balzac's death, Hańska hired Gigoux to paint a portrait of her daughter Anna; the widow and the artist lived together for the next thirty years.

Prince Soltykoff was an aristocratic Russian diplomat who retired to Paris in 1840 (age thirty-four) and embarked on an unusual second career: over the next six years he made two long voyages to the Indian subcontinent, traveling from the Himalayas to Sri Lanka and sketching the wonders he beheld. His written account of his exotic adventures and the dramatic lithographs based on his drawings caused a sensation and earned him the nickname "the Indian."

Soltykoff's pencil sketch of Félix was made in 1853, a couple of years after the triumphant Russian publication of his book—the prince was at the height of his fame. There's nothing exotic or dramatic about the portrait; it's quick, casual, and familiar. Because it's a profile, only one eye is visible—but that's the focus of the sketch. Like Gigoux, Soltykoff noticed that the bulk of Félix's energy went into looking.

Lorentz's amusing pen and ink drawing of a wild-haired photographer gives us a rare glimpse of Nadar in action, bent in half behind the camera, a bony finger in the air calling for his subject to keep still. An old friend and unreformed bohemian, Lorentz, like many others, earned the contempt of the Goncourt brothers, who called him a "caricaturist manqué" and complained of his "coarse, blunt, traveling-salesman gaiety."

Cham's cartoon portrait is weirdly unsettling. Félix's head is an explosion of orange hair and vigorous orange whiskers, and his jacket and slippers match the hair: he's a big tall orange monster

bursting through the door with an avid, pop-eyed expression on his face. "Mr. Nadar?" he asks, "C'est moi!" It's possible that the echo of Flaubert's quip about Emma Bovary is intentional. (Cham's caricatures are mentioned in Flaubert's *Sentimental Education*.) As well as evoking Félix's loud physical presence, the cartoon captures the ad hoc, constructed quality of his identity: both he and Cham were young men when they became someone else by adopting a pseudonym.

Cham's professional life was as settled and regular as can be: he worked for thirty-six years as an illustrator for Philipon's *Chari-vari*. His private life was settled, too; he ignored the tittering of snobby gossip about his domestic arrangements, as well as rumors of a veiled scandal. An elegant and refined aristocrat with a nimble intellect, he lived for twenty-five years with a woman named Jeanne Leroy, whom he always called Madame Manuel. Alexandre Dumas *fils* described her as "a fat woman, common looking, ignorant, rude, shamefully miserly, and without any wit." Dumas wondered, moreover, about her "shadowy past." But no one doubted Cham's devotion to her. When his father died in 1858, Cham inherited the title comte de Noé; eight years later, to the astonishment of his friends and family, he married Madame Manuel—which made her the comtesse de Noé. And what about *her* devotion to *him*? He died in September 1879; four months later, unable to overcome her grief, the comtesse de Noé threw herself out of a window.

———

NOTHING ABOUT THE romantic liaisons of the Dumas family was ever straightforward, which makes Dumas *fils*'s snobbery about Cham's choice of life companion all the more objectionable. Dumas *père,* himself the grandson of a French aristocrat and his African slave, had at least four illegitimate children, one of them being Dumas *fils,* who also had a child out of wedlock. (He married the mother but eventually left her for another woman.) Clearly the younger Dumas was a man with no compunction about casting the first stone.

As celebrated in his day as his father, Dumas *fils* contributed to the album a poem he wrote about a beautiful woman of dubious virtue—a woman he "studied" at length in order to write one of his highly successful plays, *Le Demi-Monde.*

———

PHILIPPE RICORD, an eminent physician, thanked Nadar for his portrait with a charmingly self-deprecating confession: "You've done better than I've ever done, for I've always found it impossible to resemble myself from one day to the next." Having studied under Baron Guillaume Dupuytren (the pioneering surgeon Félix had written about a decade earlier in his first successful feuilleton, "La Mort de Dupuytren"), Ricord specialized in venereal disease (notably disproving the erroneous theory that syphilis and gonor-rhea were caused by the same pathogen) and eventually became one of the doctors charged with the care of Napoléon III, whose urinary tract was frequently in crisis.

Félix had never lost interest in medical science, so it was a banner day for him on March 7, 1863, when he received a visit from a trio of distinguished doctors: Jules-Pierre Pelletan de Kinkelin, who wrote a book about migraines; Alexandre Brière de Boismont, author of a treatise on suicide; and Armand Trousseau, who coined the term *aphasia*.

Two years earlier Trousseau had invited Félix to photograph a hermaphrodite's "bizarre disability"—the doctor urged him to represent "her" case "in the most true and artistic manner." The result was a series of nine photographs Nadar never exhibited in his lifetime.

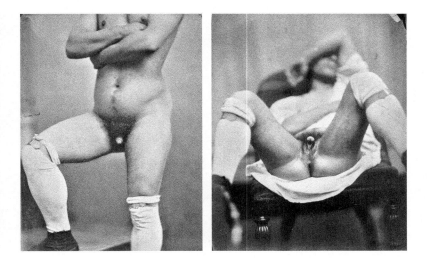

JULES SIMON, a socialist philosopher implacable in his opposition to the Second Empire, left a brief but detailed rant about the living conditions in a typical working-class household—long hours, low pay, cramped quarters—which he saw as ruinous for parents and children alike. He ended with, "And there you have the family as we have made it."

To which his fellow socialist Pierre Leroux replied, "Bravo! Monsieur Jules Simon! But how will we remake this family so badly made?" The fiery Leroux held radical ideas about the iniquity of traditional family structures. He fled France after Louis-Napoléon's coup d'état and wound up in the Channel Islands, as a near neighbor to his friend Victor Hugo, also in exile. They had long talks and frequent quarrels about socialism, art, and religion, their hearts and minds always fixed on the French capital, three hundred miles to the east.

AUGUSTE VACQUERIE and Paul Meurice, Hugo's faithful acolytes, have a page to themselves, which is as it should be. The two met as schoolboys and became inseparable friends. In 1836, while they were still at the Lycée Charlemagne in Paris, Vacquerie knocked on Hugo's door (the author lived only a few blocks away, on the place des Vosges) to deliver a long letter in verse declaring his literary ambitions. Hugo responded by inviting Vacquerie to visit; soon the young man was dining with his hero once a week and bringing along his friend Meurice.

When Hugo fled France at the end of 1851, Vacquerie followed him into exile, while Meurice remained in Paris and looked after the great man's affairs. Vacquerie's life was tangled up with Hugo's in complicated, sometimes painful ways. His older brother Charles married Hugo's daughter Léopoldine in 1843, and a few months later the newlyweds drowned in a boating accident. For many years after that tragedy, Vacquerie was the presumed fiancé of Hugo's younger daughter, the beautiful and enigmatic Adèle—but instead of marrying him, she became fixated on a British soldier whom she followed from Jersey to Nova Scotia, then to Barbados, sinking all the while into madness.

Hugo appointed Vacquerie and Meurice co-executors of his estate, and after his death in 1885, they dedicated themselves to publishing posthumous editions of his work, burnishing and sanitizing his reputation. In 1902, on the centenary of his birth, Meurice founded the Victor Hugo museum in the house on the place des

Vosges where sixty-five years earlier the famous author had entertained two star-struck schoolboys.

Vacquerie's contribution to the *livre d'or* is a dense, mournful quatrain about happiness, sorrow, sacrifice, and the unfairness of it all—four lines plucked from a poem he composed in Jersey in 1853, by which time Adèle was drifting out of reach. Who are we to begrudge him a little melancholy wallow?

Meurice, preferring a somewhat lighter tone, wrote: "The Frenchman, born clever, created vaudeville; but vaudeville, born even cleverer, destroys the Frenchman every day."

IN DECEMBER 1853, Alfred de Vigny wrote out seventy lines from the first part of his long, popular love poem called "La Maison du Berger" (The Shepherd's House). Marcel Proust, who considered Vigny and Baudelaire the two greatest French poets of the nineteenth century, was particularly fond of "La Maison du Berger"; he wrote, "In his calm poems Vigny remains mysterious, the source of his calm and its ineffable beauty escape us."

Among the lines Vigny set down in his tight, angular hand are these:

> *La distance et le temps sont vaincus. La science*
> *Trace autour de la terre un chemin triste et droit.*

> (Distance and time are vanquished. Science
> Traces around the earth a sad, straight path.)

Not an uncommon lament in the age of the railway and the steamship. It's no great surprise to see it echoed a decade later by Baron Taylor, right next to Vigny's last two stanzas. Essentially nodding in agreement with Vigny, Taylor wrote: "All the lands of our globe have now been discovered, the seas are plowed every day by our vessels, only the sky remains to be traveled."

The precise timing of Taylor's contribution is worth noting: it's dated September 20, 1863, just as Félix was making the final

preparations for the launch of *Le Géant,* his ticket to explore the
sky. Two weeks later the balloon was aloft on its maiden flight.
(And within a month, early on the morning of October 18, it had
crashed sickeningly.)

Taylor was a colossus on the Paris arts scene, a travel writer,
an impresario of the stage, an art collector who acted on behalf of
the emperor, and a philanthropist who founded a series of orga-
nizations not unlike the Société des gens de lettres (which he also
helped found), whose purpose was to support working artists of all
stripes, as well as actors, artisans, architects, inventors, and teach-
ers. Late in life he was appointed to the Senate by Napoléon III.

Art historians have spotted Taylor in Manet's *Music in the Tuile-
ries* (1862): behind two seated ladies dressed in matching gold and
blue outfits, Taylor stands with his back to us, cane under his arm,
in conversation with Baudelaire and Gautier. (Here, in the *livre
d'or,* he's also in conversation—with Vigny.)

In *Mémoires du Géant,* Félix devotes an extended digression
to Taylor's unflagging generosity and what he calls the baron's
"saintly usefulness."

———————————

AUGUSTE PRÉAULT, now hailed as the quintessential French Romantic sculptor, struggled for fifteen years without a public commission, living hand to mouth and making common cause with
Félix's band of bohemians. The Nadar portrait, made in 1854 or
1855, just as Préault's talent began to be recognized, is an expressive masterpiece, all coiled energy and ferocious intent.

Lit from above, the sculptor's head is monumental, like his
work. The fierce, narrowed eyes illustrate what Baudelaire meant
when he said that Préault had that "instinctive taste that throws
itself on beauty like an animal hunting its natural prey."

In the album, Préault wrote, "I assure you, Nadar, that ingratitude is the failure of the heart."

Henry Celliez, a lawyer who worked with Baron Taylor and
was instrumental in founding the Société des gens de lettres, added
a corollary: "Just as gratitude is the memory of the heart."

ONE OF FÉLIX'S oldest friends, André Léon-Noël, who collaborated with him on *Le Livre d'or,* the expensive literary keepsake that flickered into existence in late summer 1839 and immediately expired, left in this *livre d'or* an interminable poem written out over five pages in a patiently neat hand, with only the occasional mistake crossed out and written over.

How thoroughly bohemian was Léon-Noël? One of the more intriguing entertainments promised in the lithographed program for Félix's famous *fête champêtre* of 1840 was a sequence of *tableaux vivants* to be performed at nine o'clock by "A. Léon-Noël, poet from Orléans." Félix warned that these scenes required that the poet pose entirely naked during the entirety of the performance—but that fans and open windows would provide adequate ventilation.

Like Félix, Léon-Noël was a great friend of the man who put bohemia on the map: Henry Murger. Son of a Paris concierge who worked also as a tailor, Murger received a meager education. When he was in his twenties and already living in a garret, trying to earn a crust with his pen, he decided to spice up his name by spelling his first name in the English manner and adding a German umlaut: Henri Murger became Henry Mürger. He later dropped the umlaut. Although Murger's fiction inspired the sentimental image of bohemia bequeathed to us by Puccini's opera (impoverished young idealists dedicated to art and love), he was perfectly capable of seeing his penniless youth in a cold clear light and preferring a more comfortable lifestyle. The critical and commercial success of his tales of bohemian life, when they were adapted for the stage as *Vie de Bohème* in 1849 and published in book form in 1851, meant that he could trade his garret for a flat in town and a rented cottage in a quaint countryside village. In 1858 he was made a chevalier of the Legion of Honor, a step on the road to the Académie. But ill health and money troubles dogged him, and he died in agony at a private hospital at age thirty-eight. There's a fine monument over his grave in the Montmartre cemetery, and also a bust in the Jardin du Luxembourg, where he and Félix had spent many hours loafing. When he died, Murger was once again short of money; he left his mistress destitute. Concerned for this gentle, delicate-featured woman, a former seamstress who had lived with Murger for the last ten years of his life, Félix took up a collection that raised 250 francs, and gave her also his share of the advance for *Histoire de Mürger*. With these funds she set up an antique shop not far from Nadar's studio on the boulevard des Capucines.

For the *livre d'or*, Murger wrote out a poem from the epilogue to *Scènes de la vie de bohème*, "La chanson de Musette," a lament over the lost paradise of young love that was set to music by Alfred Vernet, who also signed the album. The multitalented Vernet was a painter who specialized in miniatures as well as an actor, a poet (he left a breezy sonnet in the *livre d'or*), and even a photographer. The melody he wrote for Murger's sad, sweet lyric was on everybody's lips; Gautier declared the song a masterpiece, "a tear that has become a pearl of poetry."

ALPHONSE KARR, Félix's boss at *Le Journal*, left a sketched self-portrait that makes him look sharp and devilish. Above the drawing he wrote out a couple of the epigrams for which he was famous:

Plus ça change, plus c'est la même chose (The more things change, the more they stay the same) and *L'amour naît de rien—et meurt de tout* (Love is born of nothing—and dies of everything).

A committed republican, Karr left Paris during the Second Empire and established himself in Nice, where he continued to write but also devoted himself to the cultivation of flowers.

The literary critic Gustave Planche ("Gustave the Cruel," as Karr called him), was a bohemian of Nerval and Gautier's generation. It was said of him that he always had a cigar in his mouth and an insult in his pen, and that as a critic he had the dexterity and the sangfroid of a surgeon. He left a barely legible, slashing remark, angling up toward the top corner of the page, about the odd things one finds in albums.

THE PRETERNATURALLY self-assured and absurdly prolific Maxime Du Camp was already well-traveled when he and his old friend Gustave Flaubert set off in the fall of 1849 on a two-year tour of Egypt and the Holy Land. Resolved to document the exotic wonders of the Orient, Du Camp had taken lessons in photography from Gustave Le Gray (as Félix's brother had done) and secured funding from the ministry of public education for an "archaeological mission." The book Du Camp published on his return is one of the first examples of travel writing illustrated with photographs. The pyramids, the sphinx, the monumental temples—he recorded the astonishing fact of their existence, which was enough to ensure the success of his book, but his photos did nothing to further the evolution of the medium. Quitting photography as suddenly as he took it up, he resumed his relentless production of prose, including a six-volume anatomy of Paris in the second half of the nineteenth century.

To the *livre d'or,* Du Camp contributed a curiously lame bon mot: "Road mender's axiom: roads are like women, it takes a lot of money to maintain them."

JACQUES OFFENBACH made use of a poem left by Henri Nicolle to improvise a jolly rustic tune, squeezing the musical notation to the left of the verses.

Fromental Halévy left a brief melody under this extravagant tribute: "When God said, let there be light! he was foreseeing Nadar."

Under Hector Berlioz's neat musical notation, Rosine Stoltz, the celebrated mezzo-soprano who played a trouser role in Berlioz's first opera, *Benvenuto Cellini*, signed her name and wrote *Honni soit qui mal y voit*, a pointed variation on the ancient motto that warns against scandal-mongering and gossip.

Well, there was plenty of scandal and gossip swirling around Stoltz, who made her debut at the Paris Opéra in Halévy's *La Juive*. A feisty prima donna with a pure voice cherished for its expressive range, she managed her glittering ten-year career at the Paris Opéra with all the usual *Sturm und Drang*, including a long affair with the director of the Opéra. Another of her many affairs was with Charles Deburau *fils*, the great mime who was photographed by Félix and Adrien—a series of images that won great acclaim and featured prominently in the fierce quarrel between the brothers.

Stoltz made herself useful to Félix at the time of the Brussels Photography Exhibition of 1856. He told Ernestine that the singer, who was performing in the city, not only helped him secure a place in the exhibition but also used her influence to get him a gold medal. The Nadar portrait of Stoltz, probably made the next year (by which time she was in her forties), is unmistakably that of a diva: the force of her personality is evident in her handsome face and long, strong neck.

Baudelaire was rumored to have been infatuated with Stoltz—or anyway that's the impression given by Félix's old friend, Théodore de Banville, who wrote a lightly fictionalized account of a twenty-something-year-old Baudelaire arriving unannounced at Stoltz's house to declare his love. The singer was out, but her maid ushered the poet into a sitting room decorated in black and white satin, with low red sofas. While he waited, he smoked furiously and composed a sinister ode about a woman murdered in a room with a refined and funereal decor very much like the one in which he found himself—the poem is clearly "A Martyr (Drawing by an Unknown Master)" from *Les Fleurs du mal*. When the singer at last appeared, the poet lashed out, "You know that I don't wish to be disturbed when I'm writing verses!"

ANOTHER WOMAN WHO signed the album (and left a punning quip about women, clothes, and what happens at forty) was Augustine Brohan, a comic actress at the Comédie-Française whose splendid career was cut short by an illness that left her nearly blind. In her retirement she married a Belgian diplomat, wrote a spirited column for *Le Figaro,* and entertained a coterie of clever friends at her weekly salon.

If that sounds disappointingly scandal-free, consider the persistent rumor that in London in the spring of 1847, she had an affair with Louis-Napoléon Bonaparte, who was at the time living the life of a English gentleman a few steps from St. James's Square. Four years later he would proclaim himself emperor of France. And when he was Napoléon III, one of his mistresses was Augustine's younger sister, Madeleine, also an actress at the Comédie-Française.

ADOLPHE THIERS, a conservative republican statesman who opposed both the socialists and Louis-Napoléon, signed his name but left no comment. On the next page is a long, singsong poem in the tight scrawl of Guillaume Guizot, son of Thiers's great rival for power, François Guizot, who was prime minister for six months before the revolution of 1848 toppled the July Monarchy. In the midst of that revolution, Louis-Philippe I offered the title of prime minister to Thiers, who prudently refused.

HENRY MONNIER, a talented illustrator who was also an actor and a playwright, left a drawing of a horse-drawn carriage with a coachman on the back—but the carriage is a man's head in profile. It's an eerie image, at once surreal and familiar.

A good friend of Balzac, Monnier served as the model for Jean-Jacques Bixiou, a caricaturist who appears in several volumes of *La Comédie humaine*. Monnier's specialty was poking fun at the bourgeoisie, especially in the person of Monsieur Prudhomme, a character he invented who was, in Balzac's words, "the illustration of the type of the Parisian middle-class."

Honoré Daumier's contribution to the *livre d'or* is a pencil drawing of Henry Monnier posing as Monsieur Prudhomme—literally
posing, with his head secured by a mechanical brace that holds it in
a fixed position. The device is a joke on the seemingly endless exposure time required by early photography and the difficulty of
holding still.

Gustave Doré, meanwhile, made a drawing of a fat cupid smoking a clay pipe—and identified it as a portrait of Daumier.

Nadar's masterful portraits of Daumier look nothing like a cupid—they're grand and solemn and charged with reverence—but the resemblance to Doré's sketch is undeniable. Note the angle of the eyebrow and the concentrated energy around the eyes.

OF THE MANY charming works of art scattered in the pages of Nadar's *livre d'or*, perhaps the most appealing is Henri Durand-Brager's "voyage around the world," a series of sixteen watercolor panels, seascapes from every corner of the globe.

Above the panels, at the top of the page, Durand-Brager included a cartoon sketch of himself with his belongings slung over his shoulder striding across the ocean, setting off on his grand adventure. At the bottom of the page, he's in quarantine, in tattered clothing, reaching out his arms to a preposterously long-legged Félix, who reaches out in turn. The peripatetic artist specialized in maritime painting—and also took some of the earliest maritime photographs.

——————— ❖ ———————

THE PROLIFIC ILLUSTRATOR and caricaturist Bertall was Félix's colleague and rival at Philipon's *Journal pour rire:* one week the cover would be Nadar's, the next week Bertall's. He also set up as a professional photographer in the same year as Félix (but later his business went bust). Bertall was short and testy, with a thick, pointed beard. And he was an aristocrat, with the cushion of family money behind him. (Bertall was a pseudonym; his real name was Charles Constant Albert Nicolas, vicomte d'Arnoux, comte de Limoges-Saint-Saëns.) There was every reason why he and Félix should have been less than friendly. And yet Bertall drew in the album a lovely, haunting image of a naked man incubating under a bell jar. Haunting and mysterious.

Who is this man in the pose of a dejected thinker, head bowed, his arms wrapped around an ink pen the size of a lance? The words JOURNAL POUR RIRE, also under the bell jar, could mean that the paper incubated an illustrator's talent. But what's the significance of the pumpkin (or whatever it is) under the second bell jar? Very possibly it's a visual pun, an in-joke we're unable to enjoy from this distance. It reminds us, in any case, that cartoonists, like clowns, can strike a desperately melancholy note.

SOMETIME AFTER 1857 (the year he inherited his father's title), John Winston Churchill, seventh duke of Marlborough, passed through Paris, visited Nadar's studio, and signed the album. The portrait Nadar made that day looks a good deal like the duke's grandson, Winston Churchill—if you can imagine Winnie with curly blond hair and magnificent muttonchop whiskers.

FÉLIX PROBABLY THOUGHT of the Duke of Marlborough as an exotic. There's no doubt that's what he thought of the three Japanese ambassadors who arrived with their translator, or of the Siamese diplomat who visited on another occasion. A rage for all things Japanese would sweep through the salons of Paris over the next few decades; Félix would have been delighted when the first secretary of the Japanese embassy left on the last page of the album a delicate ink drawing of a Far Eastern landscape.

———— ❦ ————

LÉON PAILLET WAS a journalist with a habit of doodling charmingly when he wrote letters. Here he left a cartoon of himself (holding a duck on a leash) and a goofy-looking Félix, both dressed up in Middle Eastern attire.

Alongside he left this message: "If ever, through some sort of revolution, I become the emperor of the Turks, I will make the blond Nadar my chief eunuch—with remuneration worthy of his sad post." Paillet died of cholera in 1854, a year after signing this *livre d'or.*

———— ❦ ————

NADAR'S ALBUM IS a record of celebrity. If you had yet to make your mark on the cultural life of the French capital, and weren't likely to, Félix would not have asked you to sign. It's worth noting that this elitist reflex runs counter to his radical socialist notions as well as his professed admiration for "democratic" art—"the art of the people, true art, the only art possible today." But the collecting of autographs belongs to the documentary project of the *Panthéon-Nadar*: he was rounding up illustrious contemporaries and presenting them as a cohort. Putting aside the usual nineteenth-century gender imbalance, the result shows that Félix's instincts about who to include were remarkably sharp: nearly all the hundreds of visitors who signed are traceable today, in the age of Google, and though most are forgotten (except by dedicated students of Second Empire French culture), a significant minority have a genuine claim on our attention.

Some big names are missing from this album. Victor Hugo, in exile during the reign of Napoléon III, signed a later album. Eugène Delacroix, who sat just once for Nadar, in 1858, didn't sign at all. The painter was feeling ill the day he posed and wasn't satisfied with his portrait, which makes him look haughty and sour.

Delacroix asked Félix to destroy the negative; Félix refused. Not perhaps the best moment to ask for a signature and maybe a quick sketch as well. . . .

As for George Sand, who sat for Nadar many times during the 1860s, her absence remains one of the little mysteries of this *livre d'or.*

ACKNOWLEDGMENTS

NADAR WAS A GREAT BELIEVER IN COLLABORATIVE EFFORT— so long as he retained the lion's share of the credit. I am responsible for this book (any errors are mine alone), but I couldn't have written it without the generous help of a host of others, some dear to me, some complete strangers.

My principal debt is to scholars, biographers, and curators who have devoted themselves to the study of Nadar's life and work. The catalog of the Nadar exhibition at the Musée d'Orsay and the Metropolitan Museum of Art is itself a brilliant collaborative effort, but the principal authors, Maria Morris Hambourg, Françoise Heilbrun, and Phillippe Néagu, deserve to be named individually, as do the other contributors: Sylvie Aubenas, André Jammes, Ulrich Keller, Sophie Rochard, and André Rouillé (who also produced a valuable volume of Nadar's early correspondence).

Jean Prinet and Antoinette Dilasser wrote the first Nadar biography, Roger Greaves the second, and Stéphanie de Saint Marc the third. I am indebted to them all.

Loïc Chotard wrote about Nadar's cultural milieu with great sensitivity and discernment. Elizabeth Anne McCauley, in *Industrial Madness: Commercial Photography in Paris, 1848–1971*, placed Nadar and his competitors in the context of early French photomania. Claude Malécot diligently tracked Nadar's friendship with both George Sand and Victor Hugo. The great Richard Holmes wrote about Nadar in three different books: *Footsteps*, *Sidetracks*, and *Falling Upwards*. Although he recognized Nadar as a thrilling subject, he chose not to write a biography. (Lucky me.)

Nadar's work is scattered around the world in various libraries and museums. The richest collection by far is in the Bibliothèque Nationale de France. My thanks to the friendly staff who helped me navigate the holdings of the Département des Estampes et de la Photographie. Nadar's marvelous *livre d'or*, housed at the Van Pelt Library at the University of Pennsylvania, is in the care of the Kislak Center for Special Collections, whose director, David McKnight, is kind and generous.

While I was researching and writing, the following people were helpful in ways large and small: Anthony Bailey, Kristine Baril, Anne Bazin, Laure Bazin, Peter Begley, Nathan Benn, Jane Berridge, Victoire Bourgois, Lorraine Dauleux, Emily Doucet, Julie Kavanagh, Amey Larmore, Elizabeth Eva Leach, Glenn Lowry, Michael Mattis, Max McGuinness, Stephen Pinson, Diana Pulling, Sophie Raudnitz, Hugo Rodriguez, Ashley Rountree, Beth Saunders, and Peter Spiro.

Bob Gottlieb is *perhaps* the greatest editor of all time. He read the manuscript in successive drafts and did his magic. The book would have been shorter if I'd obeyed him in every particular. But why listen to someone who may not, after all, be the greatest?

Georges Borchardt is the most agreeable of literary agents, and he is ably assisted by Samantha Shea.

Tim Duggan's name is on the spine of this book, and his generosity and friendly, level-headed intelligence were indispensable to it. Tim's assistant, William Wolfslau, is a model of cheerful (and patient) efficiency. My thanks to copyeditor Janet Biehl, cover designer Chris Brand, book designer Lauren Dong, production editor Mark McCauslin, production manager Linnea Knollmueller, indexer Nancy Wolff, publicist Sarah Grimm, and marketer Roxanne Hiatt—a publishing dream team.

This book is dedicated to my father and stepmother, Louis Begley and Anka Muhlstein. They were tireless in their support and enthusiasm for this project. Anka helped decipher the handwriting of many nineteenth-century luminaries—even over breakfast—and answered an unending stream of importuning emails. Louis read successive drafts with great care and insight.

Nothing I do would make sense without my wife, Anne Cotton, who also happens to be my first and fondest reader. Her children, Tristan and Chloë, have generously shared their mother with me for fifteen years and counting, and Chloë kindly gave me the benefit of her keen editorial eye.

Illustration Credits

All images in this book are used with permission of the following:

Bibliothèque Nationale de France, courtesy of the Gallica digital library: pages ii, 2, 3, 4, 16, 17, 21, 26, 36, 45, 47, 59, 60, 61, 69, 79, 89, 93, 94, 110, 111 (bottom), 113, 115, 117 (left), 118, 121, 128, 133 (left), 137, 140, 152, 155, 167, 169 (top and left), 173, 174, 182, 183, 189, 191, 192, 228 (bottom)

British Library: 57

Charles Patterson Van Pelt Library, courtesy of Christopher Lippa, Photographer, Schoenberg Center for Electronic Text and Image. Nadar's *Livre d'or* is housed in the Kislak Center for Special Collections, Rare Books and Manuscripts at the University of Pennsylvania: pages 197, 199, 200, 206, 208, 210, 213, 214, 215, 223, 224, 227, 228 (top), 229, 230, 232

Getty Images: page 142

Internet Archive; images digitized in 2010 with funding from the University of Ottawa: pages 53, 54, 55

J. Paul Getty Museum, courtesy of the Getty's Open Content Program: pages 63, 84, 87, 88, 111 (top), 131 (top), 132, 133 (right), 172

Library of Congress: pages 7, 136, 147 (top)

Médiathèque de l'architecture et du patrimoine/Archive photographiques: pages 169 (right), 180

Metropolitan Museum of Art, courtesy of the museum's Open Access for Scholarly Content program; www.metmuseum.com: pages 64, 66, 67, 68, 91 (right), 92 (right), 95, 108, 170, 209, 217 (right)

MoMA: pages 92 (left), 99, 116, 130, 171, 233

Musée George Sand/Ville de La Châtre: page 114

Musée du Louvre: page 190

Musée d'Orsay: pages 25, 72, 74, 77, 83, 84, 87, 91 (left), 98, 112, 117 (right), 217 (left), 221, 225

National Portrait Gallery, © National Portrait Gallery, London: page 231

Patrick Montgomery Collection: page 148

Wikimedia Commons: pages 105, 131 (bottom), 147 (bottom)

INDEX

Note: Page numbers in *italics* refer to illustrations.